hamlyn
QuickCook

hamlyn

QuickCook
One Pot

Recipes by Emma Lewis

Every dish, three ways – you choose!
30 minutes | 20 minutes | 10 minutes

An Hachette UK Company
www.hachette.co.uk

First published in Great Britain in 2012 by Hamlyn,
a division of Octopus Publishing Group Ltd
Endeavour House, 189 Shaftesbury Avenue
London WC2H 8JY
www.octopusbooks.co.uk

ISBN 978-0-600-62490-5

A CIP catalogue record for this book is available from the British Library

Printed and bound in China

10 9 8 7 6 5 4 3 2 1

Both metric and imperial measurements are given for the recipes. Use one set of
measures only, not a mixture of both.

Standard level spoon measurements are used in all recipes
1 tablespoon = 15 ml
1 teaspoon = 5 ml

Ovens should be preheated to the specified temperature. If using a fan-assisted oven,
follow the manufacturer's instructions for adjusting the time and temperature. Grills
should also be preheated.

This book includes dishes made with nuts and nut derivatives. It is advisable for
those with known allergic reactions to nuts and nut derivatives and those who may
be potentially vulnerable to these allergies, such as pregnant and nursing mothers,
invalids, the elderly, babies and children, to avoid dishes made with nuts and nut oils.

It is also prudent to check the labels of preprepared ingredients for the possible
inclusion of nut derivatives.

The Department of Health advises that eggs should not be consumed raw. This book
contains some dishes made with raw or lightly cooked eggs. It is prudent for more
vulnerable people such as pregnant and nursing mothers, invalids, the elderly, babies
and young children to avoid uncooked or lightly cooked dishes made with eggs.

Contents

Introduction

30 20 10 – Quick, Quicker, Quickest

This book offers a new and flexible approach to meal-planning for busy cooks, letting you choose the recipe option that best fits the time you have available. Inside you will find 360 dishes that will inspire and motivate you to get cooking every day of the year. All the recipes take a maximum of 30 minutes to cook. Some take as little as 20 minutes and, amazingly, many take only 10 minutes. With a bit of preparation, you can easily try out one new recipe from this book each night and slowly you will be able to build a wide and exciting portfolio of recipes to suit your needs.

How Does it Work?

Every recipe in the QuickCook series can be cooked one of three ways – a 30-minute version, a 20-minute version or a super-quick and easy 10-minute version. At the beginning of each chapter you'll find recipes listed by time. Choose a dish based on how much time you have and turn to that page.

You'll find the main recipe in the middle of the page accompanied by a beautiful photograph, as well as two time-variation recipes below.

If you enjoy your chosen dish, why not go back and cook the other time-variation options at a later date? So if you liked the 20-minute Crunchy Berry Brûlée, but only have 10 minutes to spare this time around, you'll find a way to cook it using cheat ingredients or clever shortcuts.

If you love the ingredients and flavours of the 10-minute Chilli Prawn Noodles, why not try something more substantial, like the 20-minute Chilli Prawn and Lime Couscous, or be inspired to make a more elaborate version, like the Chilli Prawn Bisque? Alternatively, browse through all 360 delicious recipes, find something that catches your eye – then cook the version that fits your time frame.

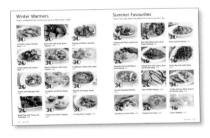

Or, for easy inspiration, turn to the gallery on pages 12–19 to get an instant overview by themes, such as Winter Warmers or Summer Favourites.

QuickCook online

To make life even easier, you can use the special code on each recipe page to email yourself a recipe card for printing, or email a text-only shopping list to your phone.

ONE-POUL-FAN

QuickCook One Pot

With so many of us living busy lives these days, cooking dinner is enough of an effort without having to tackle a mountain of dishes afterwards. One-pot dishes are simple to prepare – from an easy salad tossed together in a bowl, to quickly frying some meat and vegetables and then simmering in a flavourful liquid. Once dinner is finished the clear-up is really easy. All the recipes in this book require just one cooking utensil, and as everything is ready in just 30 minutes or less you can spend more time relaxing and less time working away in the kitchen.

Choosing the Right Dish

Casserole Dish: A heavy-based casserole dish is perfect for many one-pot dishes and there are plenty that are smart enough to bring from the hob to the table for a dinner party. They are best for making making moist dishes like stews or curries. Start off by frying meat, onions or other vegetables to get a rich base flavour, then add flavourings, maybe some tomatoes, stock or a splash of cream, cover and leave the dish to cook by itself. You can also find shallower casseroles that are great for cooking rice-based dishes. The best casseroles are made from cast iron, which is brilliant at retaining heat and ensuring even cooking. They can be pricy to buy, but they are an investment that should last you a lifetime.

Saucepan: Every cook should have a large saucepan in their kitchen. Ideally, get a heavy-based pan so you can double up and use it for frying as well. A large pan will give you the space you need to cook soup or pasta for the whole family, or any other recipe that requires a lot of liquid.

Frying pan: To give food a really robust, caramelized flavour you would find in a restaurant, you need a good sauté or frying pan. To ensure that food doesn't burn when cooking, look out for pans with a heavy base. Sticking is often a problem when frying, so try using a cast-iron pan and heating it until it is smoking hot – the heat will help prevent sticking – or you can use a nonstick pan. Sauté pans are deeper than frying pans, allowing you to fry more gently and making it easier to add a little stock or other liquid. You can also buy sauté pans with a lid, which allows you to steam food and keep it moist, or alternatively you can tightly cover the pan with tin foil. Frying pans have shallower sides and are best used when you really want to brown something over an intensive heat, like a steak.

Baking and roasting tins: Some of the simplest one-pan dishes are cooked in the oven, so after a little prep work your job is done. A simple ceramic baking dish works well and many of these are elegant enough to bring to table. But a sturdy, metal roasting tin is also useful. Try looking for versions with a handle, as this makes them easier to get out of the oven. To make sure your food gets browned in the oven, choose a tin that is shallow, otherwise the ingredients will simply steam.

Griddle pan: A griddle pan will bring all the great taste of an outdoor barbecue inside to your kitchen. The metal dish can be heated on the hob and the raised edges will give your food that special seared look. Cooking like this can be smoky, so it's worth having an extractor fan on. It's also a really healthy way to cook food. Don't add oil to the pan, rub a little oil over the surface of the food instead, then season and add to the pan. A pair of metal tongs will help you to turn over the food when it's ready. Only robust types of vegetables and meat can be griddled, otherwise they have a tendency to fall apart.

Wok: A mainstay of Asian cooking, woks are great all-round cooking utensils. You can cook large-portion meals in a wok, but make sure not to overcrowd the pan when stir-frying. Cut all the vegetables and meat to the same size so they cook quickly and evenly. Add items like noodles and rice at the end to get the maximum flavour. You can also use a wok for deep-fat frying, simmering and steaming, if it has a lid. Heavy woks are a good investment as they will ensure food doesn't burn, but nonstick versions are also available. For a gas flame, look for woks with a rounded bottom, but for electric or induction hobs, go for a wok with a flat bottom so it won't tip over during cooking.

Using the Best Ingredients

Meat: Many one-pot dishes use slower-cooking cuts taken from the shoulder or leg of the animal. These are tougher cuts and require a long and low simmering in the pot to produce tender meat. When time is of the essence you need to use quicker-cooking cuts such as loin. Taken from the middle of the animal, these cuts need to be cooked fast – if you leave them for a long time they toughen up and tend to dry out.

Ready-cooked vegetables: When you're in a hurry and want to use only one dish, there are plenty of items you should have stocked on your shelves. Ready-roasted vegetables are now widely available, and some grilled aubergine or courgettes will really lift a dish and save you lots of time and effort. They are also good to toss through a salad or finely chop to make a simple dressing or sauce.

Canned pulses: Dried beans and pulses take a long time to cook from scratch, but are perfect for absorbing delicious flavours in a dish as well as filling you up. Luckily you can find most beans canned and they are simple to drain and then wash before using. As well as being a great addition to dishes, beans and pulses make a quick and easy accompaniment – drain and pour over boiling water, then place in a processor and whizz until smooth and you'll have an instant mash. You can find lentils in cans, but they are also available in microwavable pouches, which are quick to heat through.

Ready-cooked rice and noodles: You can now buy ready-cooked rice and noodles that are simple to make into a quick one-pot supper. Cooked rice can be added or simply microwaved in the packet, while there is a large selection of noodles available to brighten up a stir-fry. Couscous, a small grain from North Africa, is the perfect quick-cooking ingredient. Measure out a mugful, add to a pan of seared meat or vegetables, then add 1.5 measures of boiling stock and cover. A couple of minutes later you'll have fluffy tender couscous to enjoy.

Prepared pastry: A crisp, rich topping of pastry makes any dinner that bit more special. Ready-made pastry is now widely available and you can also find ready-rolled pastry to make life easier still. Look out for pastry made with butter: it costs a little more, but the flavour is fantastic. In addition to puff and shortcrust pastry, try using filo pastry. These thin sheets, which crisp up in the oven, just need brushing over with melted butter or oil and can then be used to make savoury or sweet dishes.

The Finishing Touches

One-pot dishes need to be packed full of flavour, so stock up on some ingredients that will give your meals a sparkling finish.

Herbs: A handful of fresh herbs is an easy way to add fresh flavour and colour to the pot. Fresh coriander leaves will perk up ready-made curry paste, and while fresh pesto is widely available in shops, you can make your own and experiment with adding lemon juice or capers for an extra kick, or ground almonds and roasted red peppers for a Spanish-inspired taste.

Spices: Spices need a delicate touch – you don't want them to overwhelm a dish, but a pinch of something can make the most mundane meal a bit special. Paprika and dried chilli will warm up a dish, while cumin and coriander are essential to many Asian recipes. Cinnamon is very versatile and is used in many savoury dishes as well as crumbles and other puddings.

Cheese: A rich, strong cheese scattered over a dish will also help to bring it together. Feta is great for adding flavour to Greek and Mediterranean dishes, while goats' cheese also provides a nice tang. Mozzarella melts into just about any dish and sets off the sharpness of tomatoes, while a scattering of Parmesan lifts any Italian-inspired dinner.

Serve Alongside

Using just one pot makes life in the kitchen much simpler, but it's easy to also add side dishes without creating more stress. Bread is great with most meals. Choose a baguette to mop up a soupy stew, or crisp up some sliced ciabatta or bake some garlic bread to serve alongside grilled meals. Salads and Mediterranean dishes are perfect with some lightly toasted pitta bread, while it's easy to find chapattis to serve with an Indian meal.

In the warmer months, whip up a salad to enjoy with your meal. Simply whisk together one part of vinegar or lemon juice with three parts of oil and a pinch of salt, then toss together with a bag of mixed salad leaves. You can try different flavours – add a touch of mustard, some chopped herbs or a flavoured vinegar or oil if you fancy something a bit different.

Hot and Spicy

Be generous with the spices if you like your food to have that little extra kick

Chicken Pad Thai 28

Tandoori Chicken with Onions and Tomatoes 34

Chicken and Coconut Thai Curry Rice 38

Massaman Chicken Curry with Peanuts 42

Steamed Soy Chicken with Mixed Mushrooms 60

Balti Chicken and Peppers 62

Spicy Salmon with Couscous 94

Fish, Coconut and Potato Curry 106

Thai Beef Salad with Herbs 130

Sweet Potato and Coconut Curry 182

Sweetcorn, Coconut and Tomato Curry 192

Cinnamon-Spiced Cherries 240

Entertaining

Impress your guests with these delicious main courses and desserts

Chicken, Olive and Cumin Couscous 50

Seared Duck and Figs with Watercress Salad 68

Herb-Roasted Turkey Breast with Pancetta and Beans 70

Seabass with Herb and Olive Israeli Couscous 104

Baked Pancetta-Wrapped Monkfish with Tapenade 108

Rosti with Smoked Salmon and Rocket 122

Rosemary-Crusted Roast Lamb 162

Squash with Stilton Fondue 190

Crunchy Berry Brûlée 232

Boozy Caramelized Oranges 256

Tiramisu 258

Vanilla Zabaglione 278

Family Classics

A selection of recipes to please even the fussiest of young eaters

Melted Cheesy Chicken Tortilla Wedges 58

Oven-Baked Fish and Chips with Tomato Salsa 114

Roasted Sausages with Parsnips and Carrots 128

Melting Meatball Sandwiches 134

Herby Steak Tortilla Wraps 158

Italian Beefburgers with Polenta Chips 164

Fried Haloumi and Courgettes with Red Pepper Salsa 196

Pizza Fiorentina 210

Chocolate Fudge Brownie Cake 242

Choc-Chip Ice Cream Sandwiches 250

Peach and Raspberry Melba 264

Banana and Caramel Puffs 270

Soups and Stews

The ultimate one-pot meal, a warming bowl of soup or stew is always welcome

Spicy Chicken Soup with Avocado 26

French-Style Chicken Stew with Tarragon 36

Paella Soup 46

Chilli Chicken Ramen with Bean Sprouts 54

Spanish Monkfish and Clam Stew 80

Spicy Fish and Potato Soup 88

Clam, Kale and Butter Bean Stew 92

Thai Hot and Sour Prawn Soup 98

Chorizo and Black Bean Soup 148

Moroccan Lamb Stew 156

Spicy Beef and Tomato Stew with Sweetcorn 170

Pork and Paprika Goulash 172

Pasta and Noodles

Versatile, quick and popular – there's a pasta recipe to suit every taste and occasion

Sticky Lemon Chicken Noodles
32

Linguine with Creamy Chicken Carbonara 66

Chilli Prawn Noodles 86

Smoked Haddock and Watercress Cannelloni 110

Bang Bang Prawn Salad with Peanut Sauce 116

Spicy Seafood Pasta with Garlic Mayonnaise 118

Lamb Stew with Feta and Pasta 142

Stir-Fried Teriyaki Beef with Noodles and Greens 146

Creamy Ham and Tomato Penne 152

Thai Mixed Vegetable Soup 202

Red Pepper and Goats' Cheese Lasagne 204

Wintery Minestrone with Pasta and Beans 220

Pies and Tarts

A savoury pie or sweet tart makes a wonderful centrepiece for any meal

Chicken and Tomato Polenta Pie 30

Chicken and Ham Pie with Scone Topping 48

Filo-Topped Chicken, Mushroom and Dill Pie 56

Crispy Fish Pie 82

Bacon and Apple Puffs 140

Parma Ham and Asparagus Tart 144

Crispy Spinach and Feta Pie 180

Tomato and Basil Tart 184

Pastry-Topped Summer Vegetables 214

Apple and Orange Tart 234

Prune Clafoutis 260

Apricot and Almond Crostata

Winter Warmers

Hearty, wholesome fare to warm you up on a chilly winter's night

Cod with Creamy Chowder Sauce 120

Beef Stew with Garlic Bread Topping 138

Sausage and Bean Cassoulet 160

Sweet Potato and Chorizo Hash 17

Beetroot Risotto with Goats' Cheese 198

Cauliflower Cheese with Leeks 212

Tomato and Aubergine Pilaf 216

Courgette and Ricotta Bakes 222

Rhubarb and Ginger Slump 248

Baked Figs with Honey and Pistachios 252

Creamy Chocolate Puddings 268

Crunchy Pear Crumble 276

Summer Favourites

These fresh, light dishes are perfect for a sunny summer's day

2 Chicken with Warm Lentils and Kale 52

2 Rice with Salmon and Lemon Ponzu Dressing 76

3 Prawn and Pea Risotto 78

2 Steamed Lemon Dill Salmon and Potatoes 84

1 Seared Tuna with Lemon, Bean and Rocket Salad 112

1 Herby Ham and Lentil Salad 168

3 Pea and Asparagus Risotto 194

2 Feta-Stuffed Peppers 200

3 Tortilla with Sun-Blush Tomato and Rocket Salad 224

2 Strawberry Cream Puffs 236

2 Tropical Fruit Salad 244

1 Lemon Syllabub 274

QuickCook
Poultry

Recipes listed by cooking time

30

20

3⬤ Roasted Chicken with Butternut Squash

Serves 4

500 g (1 lb) butternut squash,
  peeled and cut into thin slices
1 red onion, sliced
4 bone-in chicken breasts
2 tablespoons olive oil
1 tablespoon balsamic vinegar
25 g (1 oz) walnut halves
8 sage leaves
salt and pepper

To serve

crusty bread
green salad

- Arrange the squash, onion and chicken, skin side up, in a roasting tin.

- Drizzle over the oil, season to taste and toss to make sure everything is well coated in oil. Place in a preheated oven, 200°C (400°F), Gas Mark 6, for 15 minutes.

- Drizzle over the balsamic vinegar and scatter the walnuts and sage leaves around the chicken. Return to the oven for 5–10 minutes until the squash is tender and the chicken is cooked through. Serve with crusty bread and green salad.

1⬤ Chicken, Butternut and Goats' Cheese

Pasta Cook 250 g (8 oz) peeled and diced butternut squash in a large saucepan of lightly salted boiling water for 6 minutes. Add 500 g (1 lb) fresh penne pasta and cook for a further 3 minutes, or according to the pack instructions, until 'al dente'. Add 150 g (5 oz) baby spinach leaves, then drain immediately and return the pasta and vegetables to the pan. Stir in 75 g (3 oz) soft goats' cheese and 1 ready-cooked chicken breast, torn into shreds, then season to taste and serve topped with roughly chopped walnuts.

2⬤ Chicken, Butternut and

Bean Stew Heat 2 tablespoons vegetable oil in a shallow, flameproof casserole dish. Add 300 g (10 oz) peeled and diced butternut squash and 300 g (10 oz) diced chicken breast. Season to taste and cook for 5 minutes until golden. Add 2 crushed garlic cloves, 2 finely chopped sage leaves and 200 ml (7 fl oz) hot chicken stock and bring to the boil. Reduce the heat and simmer for 12 minutes or until the chicken and squash are cooked through. Add a 200 g (7 oz) canned cannellini beans, rinsed and drained, then cook for

a further 2 minutes until heated through. Scatter with chopped parsley to serve.

Spicy Chicken Soup with Avocado

Serves 4

2 tablespoons olive oil

1 onion, chopped

3 garlic cloves, crushed

1 teaspoon chipotle peppers in adobo sauce, chopped, or Tabasco sauce

2 teaspoons sugar

400 g (13 oz) can chopped tomatoes

1 litre (1¾ pints) hot chicken stock

2 ready-cooked chicken breasts, torn into strips

1 avocado, peeled, stoned and cubed

handful of tortilla chips, crushed

4 tablespoons soured cream

handful of chopped fresh coriander

salt and pepper

- Heat the oil in a large saucepan. Add the onion and cook for 5 minutes until softened, then stir in the garlic, chipotle or Tabasco and sugar. Pour in the tomatoes and stock, bring to the boil, then reduce the heat and simmer for 10 minutes.

- Use a hand-held electric blender to purée the soup until smooth, then add a little boiling water if it is too thick and season to taste.

- Ladle the soup into bowls and scatter the chicken, avocado and tortilla chips on top. Drizzle with the soured cream and sprinkle with the coriander.

Spicy Chicken and Avocado Salad Mix a few drops of Tabasco sauce with ½ teaspoon ground cumin and 1 tablespoon olive oil. Coat 2 chicken breast fillets, cut into strips, in the oil. Cook in a hot griddle pan for 3 minutes on each side or until cooked through. Toss together 100 g (3½ oz) mixed salad leaves, 2 chopped tomatoes, 1 sliced avocado, the chicken, some crushed tortilla chips, the juice of ½ lime and 1 tablespoon olive oil.

Grilled Spicy Chicken Wings with Tomato and Avocado Salsa Mix together 1 teaspoon honey, 1 teaspoon tomato purée, ½ teaspoon ground cumin, ½ finely chopped red chilli, 1 tablespoon olive oil and 1 tablespoon lime juice in a large bowl. Season to taste, add 12 chicken wings, toss to coat and leave to marinate for 10 minutes. Cook the wings under a preheated hot grill for 5–6 minutes on each side until golden and cooked through. Roughly chop 2 avocados and 1 tomato and mix together with 1 sliced spring onion, 1 tablespoon olive oil, 1 tablespoon lime juice and a large handful of chopped fresh coriander. Season to taste and serve the salad with the hot chicken wings.

ONE-POUL-KYD

10 Chicken Pad Thai

Serves 4

3 tablespoons vegetable oil

1 egg, lightly beaten

1 garlic clove, crushed

2 teaspoons finely grated fresh
root ginger

2 spring onions, sliced

300 g (10 oz) ready-cooked rice
noodles

50 g (2 oz) bean sprouts

2 ready-cooked chicken breasts,
torn into thin strips

2 tablespoons Thai fish sauce

2 teaspoons tamarind paste

2 teaspoons sugar

pinch of chilli powder

25 g (1 oz) ready-roasted
peanuts, roughly chopped

handful of chopped fresh coriander

- Heat a large wok until smoking hot. Add 1 tablespoon of the oil and swirl around the pan, then pour in the egg. Stir around the pan and cook for 1–2 minutes until just cooked through. Remove from the wok and set aside.

- Heat the remaining oil in the wok, add the garlic, ginger and spring onions and cook for 2 minutes until softened. Add the noodles to the pan along with the bean sprouts and chicken.

- Stir in the fish sauce, tamarind paste, sugar and chilli powder and continue to cook, adding a splash of boiling water if necessary. Heat through, then return the egg to the pan and mix in. Divide between serving bowls and scatter with the peanuts and coriander to serve.

---

2 Grilled Chicken Noodle Salad

Soak 250 g (8 oz) dried rice noodles according to the pack instructions. Meanwhile, mix 2 tablespoons sweet chilli sauce with 2 tablespoons lime juice and brush over 2 skinless chicken breast fillets. Cook under a preheated medium grill for 5 minutes, turn over and cook for a further 5–7 minutes until cooked through, then slice thickly. Drain the noodles, cool under cold running water if necessary and drain again. Mix 1 teaspoon caster sugar, 2 tablespoons rice vinegar and 2 teaspoons Thai fish sauce and stir into the noodles with the chicken, 1 grated carrot, ¼ finely chopped cucumber and a large handful each of chopped fresh coriander and mint. Scatter with sesame seeds to serve.

3 Chicken Noodle Soup

Simmer 1.2 litres (2 pints) chicken stock with 3 tablespoons rice wine, 2 tablespoons light soy sauce and 1 star anise for 10 minutes. Mix 300 g (10 oz) minced chicken with 1 teaspoon grated fresh root ginger and 1 teaspoon soy sauce. Shape into balls and cook in the soup for 7 minutes. Add 100 g (3½ oz) shiitake mushrooms and cook for a further 3 minutes. Stir in 2 bok choi, quartered, and cook for 1 minute. Add 200 g (7 oz) ready-cooked rice noodles, heat through and serve.

ONE-POUL-KID

30 Chicken and Tomato Polenta Pie

Serves 4

2 tablespoons olive oil

300 g (10 oz) skinless chicken breast fillets, diced

2 garlic cloves, finely chopped

1 teaspoon tomato purée

400 g (13 oz) can chopped tomatoes

pinch of dried chilli flakes

handful of chopped basil

1 courgette, sliced

500 g (1 lb) ready-cooked polenta, cut into 1 cm (½ inch) slices

25 g (1 oz) Parmesan cheese, grated

salt and pepper

- Heat the oil in a shallow, flameproof casserole dish. Add the chicken, season to taste and cook for 3–4 minutes until starting to turn golden, then remove from the dish and set aside.

- Add the garlic to the dish, cook for 1 minute, then pour in the tomatoes. Stir in the chilli and basil, bring to the boil, then reduce the heat and simmer for 10 minutes.

- Return the chicken to the dish along with the courgette and cook for a further 5–10 minutes until the chicken is just cooked through.

- Arrange the polenta slices on top of the chicken mixture, then scatter over the Parmesan. Cook under a preheated hot grill for 5 minutes or until golden and bubbling.

 Sweetcorn, Tomato and Chicken Salad
Heat 1 tablespoon olive oil in a frying pan. Add 75 g (3 oz) fresh or canned sweetcorn kernels and cook for 3 minutes until browned. Chop 1 cos lettuce and toss with 2 chopped tomatoes and 2 ready-cooked chicken breasts, torn into shreds. Mix 50 ml (2 fl oz) buttermilk with 1 teaspoon cider vinegar and 1 teaspoon sugar and season to taste. Scatter the sweetcorn over the salad, then drizzle over the buttermilk dressing and serve immediately.

 Griddled Polenta with Chicken and Tomatoes Heat a griddle pan until smoking hot. Rub 1 tablespoon olive oil over 4 boneless, skinless chicken breasts. Season to taste and cook for 5–7 minutes on each side until just cooked through. Cut into thick slices and toss with 4 chopped tomatoes, 1 tablespoon sherry vinegar, 3 tablespoons extra virgin olive oil and a large handful of chopped fresh basil. Cut 500 g (1 lb) ready-cooked polenta into thick slices. Brush a little oil on each slice, then cook in the griddle pan for 2 minutes on each side until charred. Spoon the warm chicken mixture over the polenta to serve.

Sticky Lemon Chicken Noodles

Serves 4

2 tablespoons vegetable oil
300 g (10 oz) chicken fillets, cut
　into thin strips
200 g (7 oz) Tenderstem broccoli
2 garlic cloves, crushed
2 teaspoons finely grated fresh
　root ginger
1 red chilli, finely chopped
finely grated rind and juice of
　1 lemon
1 tablespoon runny honey
2 teaspoons light soy sauce
300 g (10 oz) ready-cooked egg
　noodles
handful of roasted cashew nuts

- Heat a wok until smoking hot, then pour in the oil, swirl around the pan and add the chicken. Cook for 1 minute, then add the broccoli and cook for 5 minutes until the chicken is nearly cooked through.

- Add the garlic, ginger and chilli to the wok and cook for a further 1 minute. Then add the lemon rind and juice, the honey and soy sauce and toss around the pan.

- Add the noodles and a splash of water and cook until heated through. Divide between serving bowls, scatter over the cashew nuts and serve.

 ### Roasted Lemon Chicken with

Broccoli Mix together 1 teaspoon ground cumin, 1 teaspoon runny honey, 1 crushed garlic clove and 3 tablespoons olive oil. Stir in the finely grated rind of 1 lemon and a squeeze of lemon juice and season to taste. Place 4 chicken breast fillets and 200 g (7 oz) Tenderstem broccoli in a roasting tin. Pour over the lemon mixture and toss well. Place in a preheated oven, 200°C (400°F), Gas Mark 6, for 15 minutes or until the chicken is cooked through. Sprinkle over some sesame seeds and serve with boiled rice.

Lemon Chicken Risotto

Heat 1 tablespoon olive oil in a large saucepan. Add 1 finely chopped shallot and 1 crushed garlic clove and cook for 5 minutes until softened. Stir in 325 g (11 oz) risotto rice followed by 100 ml (3½ fl oz) dry white wine and bubble until boiled away. Gradually add 1 litre (1¾ pints) hot chicken stock, a ladleful at a time, stirring continuously and allowing each ladleful to be absorbed before adding the next. After 15 minutes, add 2 ready-cooked chicken breasts, torn into strips. Stir in the finely grated rind of 1 lemon and cook for a further 2 minutes or until the rice is tender, then add a squeeze of lemon juice. Season to taste and spoon into serving bowls, then spoon 75 g (3 oz) mascarpone cheese on top and add a handful of rocket to each portion.

30 Tandoori Chicken with Onions and Tomatoes

Serves 4

4 skinless chicken breast fillets
100 ml (3½ fl oz) natural yogurt
1 garlic clove, crushed
2 teaspoons finely grated fresh
root ginger
2 tablespoons tandoori curry
paste
1 onion, cut into wedges
2 tablespoons vegetable oil
2 tomatoes, quartered
15 g (½ oz) butter, cut into small
pieces
salt and pepper

To serve

lime wedges
ready-made raita
naan breads

- Line a baking sheet with foil and set a wire rack on top. Make 3 slashes across each chicken breast. Mix together the yogurt, garlic, ginger and tandoori paste and season well. Rub all over the chicken and leave to marinate for 5–10 minutes.

- Toss the onion and chicken with the oil, then arrange on the rack. Place in a preheated oven, 230°C (450°F), Gas Mark 8, for 7 minutes.

- Add the tomatoes, scatter over the butter and return to the oven for a further 5–10 minutes until the chicken is charred and just cooked through. Serve with lime wedges, raita and naan.

10 Easy Tandoori Chicken Curry

Heat 1 tablespoon vegetable oil in a large, heavy-based saucepan. Add 1 crushed garlic clove and 1 teaspoon finely grated fresh root ginger and cook for 1 minute, then stir in 2 teaspoons tomato purée and 1 tablespoon curry powder. Add a 200 g (7 oz) can chopped tomatoes and simmer for 5 minutes. Add 400 g (13 oz) ready-cooked tandoori chicken mini-fillets and 50 ml (2 fl oz) double cream. Heat until piping hot, then serve with naan bread.

20 Tandoori Chicken Skewers

Cut 300 g (10 oz) boneless, skinless chicken thighs into chunks. Mix 50 ml (2 fl oz) natural yogurt with 1 teaspoon paprika, 1 teaspoon ground cumin and ½ teaspoon ground coriander. Add a squeeze of lemon juice, then use to coat the chicken chunks. Thread the chicken on to metal skewers, alternating with onion wedges and cherry tomatoes. Heat a griddle pan until smoking hot, brush 1 tablespoon oil over the skewers, then cook for

5–7 minutes on each side until charred and cooked through. Scatter with chopped fresh coriander and serve on warmed chapattis.

 # French-Style Chicken Stew with Tarragon

Serves 4

1 leek, sliced

4 boneless, skinless chicken thighs, cut into chunks

400 g (13 oz) small new potatoes, halved

1 carrot, sliced

400 ml (14 fl oz) hot chicken stock

50 ml (2 fl oz) dry white wine

100 g (3½ oz) frozen peas, defrosted

2 tablespoons crème fraîche

salt and pepper

handful of chopped tarragon, to serve

- Place the leek, chicken, potatoes and carrot in a large saucepan. Pour in the stock and wine and season to taste.

- Bring to the boil, then reduce the heat and simmer for 15 minutes until just cooked through.

- Stir in the peas and crème fraîche and heat through. Scatter over the tarragon and serve immediately.

 Chicken Sauté with Peas, Lettuce and Tarragon Heat 1 tablespoon oil in a saucepan. Add 300 g (10 oz) thinly sliced chicken and cook for 2 minutes until golden. Add 1 crushed garlic clove and cook for a further 30 seconds. Pour in 25 ml (1 fl oz) dry white wine and bubble for 1 minute, then add 50 ml (2 fl oz) chicken stock and boil hard for 2 minutes. Stir in 100 g (3½ oz) defrosted frozen peas, 1 sliced Little Gem lettuce and 2 tablespoons crème fraîche, season to taste and heat through. Sprinkle with chopped tarragon and serve with lightly toasted baguette slices.

 Steamed Tarragon Chicken Parcels Cut 4 large squares of nonstick baking paper. Place 1 small skinless chicken breast fillet on each. Divide 4 thickly sliced baby leeks and 8 baby carrots, halved lengthways, between the parcels and place a slice of butter and a sprig of tarragon on top of each chicken breast. Season to taste, fold the paper over and roll up the edges to create airtight parcels, leaving just a little gap. Pour 25 ml (1 fl oz) dry white wine into each parcel and then fully seal, leaving enough space in the packages for air to circulate. Place on a baking sheet and cook in a preheated oven, 220°C (425°F), Gas Mark 7, for 20 minutes or until cooked through. Serve with boiled rice, if liked.

3⟐ Chicken and Coconut Thai Curry Rice

Serves 4

1 tablespoon vegetable oil
1 onion, finely chopped
1 garlic clove, crushed
2 teaspoons finely grated fresh
   root ginger
2 tablespoons Thai green curry
   paste
325 g (11 oz) chicken mini-fillets
1 red pepper, cored, deseeded and
   thickly sliced
250 g (8 oz) jasmine rice
400 ml (14 fl oz) coconut milk
300 ml (½ pt) chicken stock
salt and pepper
handful of chopped basil, to garnish
lime wedges, to serve

- Heat the oil in a large, flameproof casserole dish or heavy-based saucepan. Add the onion and cook for 5 minutes until softened. Stir in the garlic, ginger and curry paste and cook for a further 1 minute. Add the chicken and red pepper, followed by the rice, and stir well.

- Pour in the coconut milk and stock and season to taste. Bring to the boil, then reduce the heat and simmer for about 10 minutes until nearly all the liquid has boiled away.

- Turn the heat down as low as it will go, cover the pan and cook for a further 5 minutes or until the rice is cooked through. Sprinkle over the basil and serve the rice hot with lime wedges for squeezing.

 Stir-Fried Thai Chicken with Coconut Milk Heat a wok, then add 2 tablespoons vegetable oil. Add 1 sliced shallot and cook for 1 minute, then add 325 g (11 oz) chicken mini-fillets. Stir-fry for 5 minutes until the chicken is nearly cooked through. Add 1 crushed garlic clove and 1 teaspoon finely grated fresh root ginger and cook for 1 minute. Add 2 tablespoons Thai fish sauce, 2 teaspoons sugar, 75 g (3 oz) cherry tomatoes and 100 ml (3½ fl oz) coconut milk and simmer for 1 minute until the chicken is cooked through. Serve with rice noodles.

 Spicy Coconut and Chicken Soup Heat 1 tablespoon oil in a large, heavy-based saucepan. Add 2 finely chopped shallots and cook for 2 minutes to soften. Stir in 2 teaspoons finely grated fresh root ginger and 2 tablespoons Thai green curry paste. Cook for a further 1 minute, then add 400 ml (14 fl oz) coconut milk, 1 litre (1¾ pints) hot chicken stock, 2 tablespoons Thai fish sauce, 2 teaspoons sugar, 1 lemon grass stalk and 2 kaffir lime leaves. Bring to the boil, then reduce the heat and simmer for 10 minutes. Stir in 2 ready-cooked chicken breasts, torn into shreds, 300 g (10 oz) ready-cooked rice noodles and 150 g (5 oz) canned bamboo shoots and simmer until heated through. Ladle into bowls and serve sprinkled with bean sprouts, finely chopped red chilli and fresh coriander leaves.

20 Chicken Breasts with Mascarpone Cheese and Tomatoes

Serves 4

3 tablespoons olive oil, plus extra
for greasing
4 tablespoons mascarpone
cheese
4 teaspoons fresh green pesto
4 skinless chicken breast fillets
100 g (3½ oz) dried breadcrumbs
150 g (5 oz) cherry tomatoes
25 g (1 oz) toasted pine nuts
salt and pepper
crusty bread, to serve (optional)

- Mix together the mascarpone and pesto. Use a small, sharp knife to make a horizontal slit in the side of each chicken breast to form a pocket. Fill the pockets with the mascarpone mixture.

- Season the chicken and rub with 1 tablespoon of the oil then turn in the breadcrumbs until well coated. Place in a baking tray, drizzle over another tablespoon of oil and cook in a preheated oven, 200°C (400°F), Gas Mark 6, for 10 minutes.

- Add the tomatoes to the baking sheet, season and drizzle with the remaining oil. Return to the oven for a further 5 minutes or until the chicken is cooked through. Scatter over the pine nuts and serve with crusty bread, if liked.

---

10 Chicken Pizza Melts with Cheese and Tomatoes Cut 2 skinless chicken breast fillets in half horizontally and place on a lightly greased baking sheet. Top each with a slice of tomato and a slice of mozzarella cheese, then season to taste. Cook under a preheated hot grill for 7 minutes or until the cheese has melted and the chicken is cooked through. Serve in burger buns with a few salad leaves.

30 Roasted Chicken with Goats' Cheese and Tomatoes Ease the skin away from 4 bone-in chicken breasts to create a small pocket, making sure the skin is still attached on 3 sides. Cut 75 g (3 oz) soft goats' cheese into 4 thick slices. Tuck a slice of cheese under the skin of each chicken breast and top with a sprig of thyme. Place in a lightly greased large roasting tin with 4 unpeeled garlic cloves. Place in a preheated oven, 200°C (400°F), Gas Mark 6, for 15 minutes. Remove the garlic cloves and squeeze out the flesh. Tip a 400 g (13 oz) can chopped tomatoes into the tin, stir in the garlic and season well. Return to the oven for a further 5 minutes, then add a 400 g (13 oz) can cannellini beans, rinsed and drained. Cook for a further 3–5 minutes until the beans are hot and the chicken is cooked through, then serve.

30 Massaman Chicken Curry with Peanuts

Serves 4

1 tablespoon vegetable oil

4 boneless, skinless chicken thighs, cut into chunks

2 tablespoons massaman curry paste

3 tablespoons smooth peanut butter

150 ml (¼ pint) coconut milk

150 ml (¼ pint) chicken stock

1 lemon grass stalk

1 tablespoon Thai fish sauce

2 teaspoons brown sugar

2 large waxy potatoes, peeled and cut into chunks

salt and pepper

handful of chopped fresh coriander

handful of roasted peanuts, roughly chopped

- Heat the oil in a large saucepan or wok. Add the chicken and cook for 7 minutes until golden. Add the curry paste and stir to coat. Stir in the peanut butter, coconut milk and stock, season to taste and stir well.

- Add the lemon grass, fish sauce, sugar and potatoes, bring to the boil, then reduce the heat and simmer for 15 minutes or until the chicken and potatoes are cooked through. Spoon into bowls, scatter over the coriander and peanuts and serve hot.

 Stir-Fried Chicken with Peanuts

Heat 1 tablespoon vegetable oil in a wok. Add 2 tablespoons raw peanuts and cook for 2 minutes. Remove from the pan and add 1 sliced shallot and 300 g (10 oz) sliced chicken breast. Stir-fry for 2 minutes, then add 1 crushed garlic clove, 1 teaspoon grated fresh root ginger and 100 g (3½ oz) halved cherry tomatoes. Toss, then add 1 tablespoon Thai fish sauce, 1 teaspoon sugar and 300 g (10 oz) ready-cooked rice noodles. Stir well, then add the peanuts and a squeeze of lime.

 Peanut and Massaman Chicken Thighs Brush 1 tablespoon vegetable oil and 1 teaspoon massaman curry paste over 4 boneless, skinless chicken thighs. Place on a baking sheet and cook in a preheated oven, 200°C (400°F), Gas Mark 6, for 10 minutes. Mix 2 teaspoons massaman curry paste with 6 tablespoons peanut butter and 3 tablespoons coconut milk or water. Drizzle 2 tablespoons of the mixture over the chicken and return to the oven for a further 5 minutes or until the chicken is cooked through. Place the remaining sauce in a dipping bowl and serve with the chicken, with slices of cucumber, plenty of prawn crackers and boiled rice, if liked.

Citrus-Griddled Chicken with Hummus and Pitta

Serves 4

2 teaspoons ground sumac (optional)

handful of thyme leaves, finely chopped

finely grated rind and juice of 1 lemon

1½ tablespoons olive oil

4 boneless, skinless chicken thighs

4 pitta breads

salt and pepper

To serve

rocket leaves

ready-made hummus

- Mix the sumac, thyme and grated lemon rind with the olive oil. Season to taste, then rub all over the chicken and set aside for 5 minutes.

- Heat a griddle pan until smoking hot. Cook the pitta breads for 1–2 minutes on each side until lightly browned, then set aside.

- Cook the chicken thighs for 4–5 minutes on each side until lightly charred and cooked through. Squeeze a little lemon juice over the rocket and divide between serving plates. Cut the chicken into pieces and arrange on the plates with a spoonful of hummus and the pitta breads, torn into strips.

 Seared Chicken with Chickpeas and Pitta Breads Heat 1 tablespoon olive oil in a frying pan. Add 300 g (10 oz) diced chicken breast and cook for 5 minutes until golden. Stir in 1 finely chopped garlic clove and 1 teaspoon ground cumin. Add a 400 g (13 oz) can chickpeas, rinsed and drained, to the pan along with 50 ml (2 fl oz) chicken stock. Season to taste and simmer for 3–4 minutes until the chicken is cooked through. Sprinkle over 1 teaspoon ground sumac and a handful of chopped parsley, then serve with warmed pitta breads.

 Hummus-Crumbed Chicken in Pitta Pockets Spread 100 g (3½ oz) hummus over 4 skinless chicken breast fillets. Place 100 g (3½ oz) dried breadcrumbs on a plate. Mix in the finely grated rind of 1 lemon and 1 teaspoon ground sumac. Roll the chicken in the breadcrumbs until well coated. Place on a baking sheet and drizzle over 2 tablespoons olive oil. Place in a preheated oven, 200°C (400°F), Gas Mark 6, for 15 minutes or until cooked through. Cut the chicken into slices and serve inside pitta breads with some tomato slices and rocket.

ONE-POUL-CUF

2🕐 Paella Soup

Serves 4

1 tablespoon olive oil

1 onion, finely chopped

250 g (8 oz) chorizo, chopped

2 garlic cloves, crushed

200 g (7 oz) can chopped
    tomatoes

1 litre (1¾ pints) chicken stock

pinch of saffron threads

2 skinless chicken breast fillets,
    cubed

1 red pepper, cored, deseeded
    and chopped

250 g (8 oz) ready-cooked rice

50 g (2 oz) frozen peas, defrosted

salt and pepper

- Heat the oil in a large, heavy-based saucepan. Add the onion and chorizo and cook for 2 minutes or until the onion has softened and the chorizo is lightly browned.

- Stir in the garlic, then add the tomatoes, stock and saffron, and season to taste. Bring to the boil, add the chicken and red pepper and simmer for 10–12 minutes or until the chicken is cooked through.

- Add the rice and peas and cook for 2–3 minutes until heated through. Ladle the soup into bowls and serve.

1🕐 Chicken, Chorizo and Tomato Skewers Toss 300 g (10 oz) diced skinless chicken breast fillet and 100 g (3½ oz) cherry tomatoes in 2 tablespoons olive oil and season well. Cut 250 g (8 oz) chorizo into thick slices. Thread the chicken, tomatoes and chorizo on to metal skewers and cook under a preheated hot grill for 3–5 minutes on each side or until cooked through. Serve in lightly toasted baguettes with a handful of rocket.

 Chicken, Chorizo and Prawn Paella Heat 1 tablespoon oil in a frying pan. Add 250 g (8 oz) chopped chorizo and cook for 3 minutes until browned, then remove from the pan and set aside. Add 1 finely chopped onion and 4 diced boneless, skinless chicken thighs to the pan and cook for 2 minutes. Stir in 2 crushed garlic cloves and 250 g (8 oz) paella rice. Add 1 cored, deseeded and sliced green pepper and the chorizo. Pour in 750 ml (1¼ pints) chicken stock and a pinch of saffron threads and cook for 10 minutes. Stir in 100 g (3½ oz) large raw, peeled prawns and cook for a further 5–10 minutes until the rice is tender and the prawns are cooked through. Serve scattered with chopped parsley.

3 Chicken and Ham Pie with Scone Topping

Serves 4

2 tablespoons butter

2 leeks, sliced

300 g (10 oz) skinless, boneless
chicken thighs, diced

150 g (5 oz) piece of ham, cut
into small chunks

150 ml (¼ pint) hot chicken stock

100 ml (3½ fl oz) crème fraîche

150 g (5 oz) plain flour

1 tablespoon baking powder

2 tablespoons olive oil

150 ml (¼ pint) milk

2 tablespoons mixed herbs (such
as parsley, thyme, chives), finely
chopped

25 g (1 oz) Cheddar cheese,
grated

salt and pepper

- Melt the butter in a shallow, flameproof casserole dish. Add the leeks and cook for 3 minutes until softened. Add the chicken and cook for 2 minutes until lightly browned all over. Stir in the ham, stock and crème fraîche, then season to taste.

- Mix the flour and baking powder in a bowl, then pour in the oil and milk. Mix gently, season well and stir in the herbs and cheese.

- Arrange spoonfuls of the dough on top of the chicken mixture, leaving a little space between each spoonful. Place in a preheated oven, 220°C (425°F), Gas Mark 7, for 15–20 minutes until the topping is lightly browned and the chicken is cooked through.

 1 Creamy Chicken and Ham Pasta

Cook 400 g (13 oz) quick-cook spaghetti in a large saucepan of lightly salted boiling water according to the pack instructions, adding 1 finely sliced leek for the last 5 minutes of cooking. Drain and return the pasta and leek to the pan. Stir in 2 ready-cooked chicken breasts, torn into shreds, and 4 slices of ham, torn into strips. Season well, add 4 tablespoons crème fraîche, then scatter with chopped parsley to serve.

 2 Scones with Chicken and Ham

Place 325 g (11 oz) plain flour in a food processor with 75 g (3 oz) cold butter, cut into cubes, 1 teaspoon baking powder, 150 ml (¼ pint) buttermilk and a pinch of salt. Blend until a smooth dough forms. Knead in 2 finely chopped spring onions. Turn the dough on to a lightly floured surface and roll out to about 2 cm (¾ inch) thick. Use a 7 cm (3 inch) round cutter to cut out about 8 scones, re-rolling the trimmings to make more scones. Place on a floured baking sheet and cook in a preheated oven, 220°C (425°F), Gas Mark 7, for about 12 minutes until just cooked through. Split the scones and place a slice of ham and a slice of ready-cooked chicken inside each. Top with shredded lettuce and a spoonful of mayonnaise.

10 Chicken, Olive and Cumin Couscous

Serves 4

4 tablespoons olive oil
½ lemon (rind and flesh), finely chopped
1 tablespoon runny honey
½ teaspoon ground cumin
1 garlic clove, crushed
300 g (10 oz) couscous
300 ml (½ pint) hot chicken stock
400 g (13 oz) can chickpeas, rinsed and drained
50 g (2 oz) green olives, pitted
2 ready-cooked chicken breasts, sliced
handful each of chopped fresh coriander and mint
salt and pepper

- Heat the oil and lemon in a saucepan and cook over a gentle heat for about 2 minutes until the lemon is soft.

- Stir in the honey, cumin and garlic and heat through. Stir in the couscous, stock, chickpeas, olives and chicken.

- Remove from the heat and leave for 5 minutes until the couscous is tender. Fluff up with a fork and stir in the coriander and mint. Season to taste and serve immediately.

2 Cumin-Dusted Chicken Breasts with Spicy Olive Couscous

Heat 2 tablespoons oil in a frying pan. Dust 4 small chicken breast fillets with 1 teaspoon ground cumin, season and cook for 5 minutes on each side until just cooked through. Stir in 1 crushed garlic clove and 2 teaspoons harissa or chilli paste. Add 250 g (8 oz) couscous, 300 ml (½ pint) hot chicken stock and 50 g (2 oz) green olives. Cover and leave for 5 minutes until the couscous is tender. Fluff up with a fork and stir in a handful each of chopped mint and fresh coriander and the grated rind and juice of ½ lemon.

3 Chicken Stewed with Peppers, Olives and Cumin

Mix together 2 tablespoons olive oil, 3 crushed garlic cloves, 1 teaspoon ground cumin, ½ teaspoon ground turmeric, a pinch of chilli powder, 4 tablespoons lemon juice, 2 handfuls of finely chopped fresh coriander and a handful of finely chopped parsley. Rub most of the paste over 4 skinless chicken breast fillets. Heat 2 tablespoons olive oil in a deep frying pan with a lid. Add 400 g (13 oz) sliced new potatoes and cook for 5 minutes until starting to colour. Stir in the remaining herb paste with 1 cored, deseeded and chopped green pepper, then place the chicken on top. Pour in 100 ml (3½ fl oz) chicken stock and cover the pan tightly. Cook over a low heat for 20 minutes or until cooked through. Serve with steamed couscous, if liked.

20 Chicken with Warm Lentils and Kale

Serves 4

2 tablespoons olive oil

4 skinless chicken breast fillets

1 garlic clove, sliced

100 g (3½ oz) kale, chopped

250 g (8 oz) can Puy lentils, rinsed and drained

2 tablespoons lemon juice

75 g (3 oz) sun-blush tomatoes

75 g (3 oz) soft goats' cheese, crumbled

salt and pepper

- Heat half the oil in a large frying pan. Add the chicken, season to taste and cook for 5 minutes, then turn over and cook for 2 minutes until golden all over.

- Add the remaining oil to the pan along with the garlic, kale and a splash of water. Cover and cook for 7 minutes until the kale is tender and the chicken cooked through.

- Stir in the lentils and heat through, then add the lemon juice and tomatoes. Check and adjust the seasoning if necessary. Cut the chicken into thick slices and arrange on plates with the lentils. Scatter over the goats' cheese and serve immediately.

 Lentil, Kale and Chicken Bruschetta

Cook 50 g (2 oz) finely chopped kale in a pan of lightly salted boiling water for 5–7 minutes until tender. Add 100 g (3½ oz) canned Puy lentils, rinsed and drained, for the last minute of cooking, then drain well. Spread 75 g (3 oz) soft goats' cheese over 8 thick slices of toasted ciabatta. Mix the warm lentils with 2 teaspoons balsamic vinegar, 2 tablespoons olive oil and 25 g (1 oz) chopped sun-dried tomatoes, season to taste and spoon on to the toasts. Tear 1 ready-cooked chicken breast into strips and arrange on top, then drizzle with 1 tablespoon walnut oil and scatter over a handful of toasted walnut halves.

 Hearty Lentil, Kale and Chicken Soup

Heat 2 tablespoons olive oil in a saucepan. Add 1 finely chopped onion and cook gently for 5 minutes, then add 2 chopped garlic cloves, 1 teaspoon tomato purée and a pinch of dried chilli flakes and cook for a further 1 minute. Pour in 1.8 litres (3 pints) chicken stock and bring to the boil. Add 150 g (5 oz) dried red lentils and simmer for 5 minutes. Skim off any scum that rises to the surface, add 200 g (7 oz) diced chicken breast and cook for a further 5 minutes. Add 100 g (3½ oz) chopped kale and simmer for 7 minutes until tender. Season to taste and serve in warmed bowls with crusty bread.

 # Chilli Chicken Noodle Soup

Serves 4

1.2 litres (2 pints) hot chicken stock
1 tablespoon chilli sauce
2 teaspoons Thai fish sauce
1 teaspoon soy sauce
2 teaspoons rice vinegar
2 teaspoons mirin
2 skinless chicken breast fillets
300 g (10 oz) ramen or ready-cooked egg noodles
2 bok choi, quartered
75 g (3 oz) bean sprouts
1 red chilli, sliced
handful of chopped fresh coriander
lime wedges, to serve

- Pour the stock into a large saucepan, add the chilli sauce, fish sauce, soy sauce, rice vinegar and mirin and bring to the boil. Reduce to a simmer, then add the chicken breasts and cook for 10–15 minutes until just cooked through. Remove from the pan and cut into thick slices.

- Add the noodles and bok choi to the pan and cook for 2 minutes or until tender and heated through. Ladle the soup into bowls. Arrange the chicken on top, then scatter over the bean sprouts, chilli and coriander and serve with lime wedges.

 ### Spicy Chicken Soup in a Cup

Heat 600 ml (1 pint) chicken stock in a saucepan to boiling point. Add 1 teaspoon chilli sauce, 2 teaspoons soy sauce, 200 g (7 oz) ready-cooked egg noodles, 1 ready-cooked chicken breast, torn into shreds, 50 g (2 oz) baby spinach leaves and 50 g (2 oz) bean sprouts. Divide between large cups and top each serving with a sprinkling of sesame seeds.

 ### Teriyaki Chicken with Noodles

Mix together 5 tablespoons soy sauce, 5 tablespoons mirin, 1 tablespoon caster sugar, 1 crushed garlic clove and 1 teaspoon finely grated fresh root ginger. Add 400 g (13 oz) diced boneless, skinless chicken thighs, toss to coat and leave to marinate for 10 minutes. Heat 3 tablespoons vegetable oil in a wok. Add 1 sliced shallot and stir-fry for 1 minute. Remove the chicken from the marinade, add to the wok and stir-fry for 5 minutes. Add 1 cored, deseeded and sliced red pepper and stir-fry for about a further 5 minutes until the chicken is cooked through. Add 300 g (10 oz) ready-cooked egg noodles, 75 g (3 oz) bean sprouts and the marinade and heat through until piping hot before serving.

Filo-Topped Chicken, Mushroom and Dill Pie

Serves 4

1 tablespoon vegetable oil
1 onion, finely chopped
300 g (10 oz) skinless chicken breast fillets, diced
150 g (5 oz) mushrooms, halved if large
3 tablespoons dry white wine
5 tablespoons crème fraîche
finely grated rind of 1 lemon
handful of chopped dill
3 large filo pastry sheets
40 g (1½ oz) butter, melted
salt and pepper

- Heat the oil in a shallow, ovenproof casserole dish. Add the onion and cook for 2 minutes, then stir in the chicken and cook for a further 5 minutes. Add the mushrooms and continue to cook for 1 minute until starting to soften.

- Pour in the wine, cook until it has bubbled away, then stir in the crème fraîche, lemon rind and dill and remove from the heat. Season to taste.

- Meanwhile, unwrap the filo pastry and cover with a piece of damp kitchen paper until ready to use it. Working quickly, brush 1 sheet with melted butter and cut into 3 long strips. Arrange the strips on top of the chicken, scrunching it up a little. Repeat with the remaining pastry until the chicken is covered.

- Brush all over with any remaining butter, then place in a preheated oven, 200°C (400°F), Gas Mark 6, for 15–20 minutes until the filo pastry is crisp and the chicken is cooked through.

10 **Chicken and Wild Mushrooms in a Creamy Dill Sauce** Heat 1 tablespoon olive oil in a frying pan. Add 1 sliced onion and cook for 5 minutes until softened. Stir in 1 crushed garlic clove and 150 g (5 oz) mixed wild mushrooms. Cook for 3 minutes, then add 2 ready-cooked chicken breasts, torn into shreds, 3 tablespoons crème fraîche and 2 tablespoons chicken stock. Heat through, then add a handful of chopped dill and a good squeeze of lemon juice. Serve with garlic bread.

20 **Chicken, Mushroom and Dill Strudels** Mix together 1 crushed garlic clove and 2 tablespoons olive oil. Toss with 150 g (5 oz) halved mushrooms, place on a baking sheet and cook in a preheated oven, 200°C (400°F), Gas Mark 6, for 3–5 minutes. Meanwhile, brush 50 g (2 oz) melted butter over 4 filo pastry sheets. Arrange ½ ready-cooked chicken breast, torn into shreds, at one short end of each piece of pastry. Spoon over 1 tablespoon crème fraîche, a little grated lemon rind and some chopped dill. Sprinkle the cooked mushrooms on top, then fold over the long sides and roll up the pastry. Place the parcels on the baking sheet and brush with more butter. Cook in the oven for 10–15 minutes until golden and crisp.

1 Melted Cheesy Chicken Tortilla Wedges

Serves 4

8 corn or wheat tortillas

2 ready-cooked chicken breasts, torn into shreds

2 ready-roasted red peppers, torn into strips

1 red chilli, finely chopped

100 g (3½ oz) chorizo, thinly sliced

200 g (7 oz) mozzarella cheese, thinly sliced

50 g (2 oz) mature Cheddar cheese, grated

handful of chopped fresh coriander

salt and pepper

ready-made guacamole, to serve

- Lay 4 tortillas on 2 large baking sheets and scatter with the chicken, red peppers and chilli. Divide the chorizo and cheese between the tortillas and sprinkle over the coriander.

- Season to taste, place another tortilla on top of each to make a sandwich, then gently press down with your hand.

- Place in a preheated oven, 190°C (375°F), Gas Mark 5, and cook for 7 minutes until lightly crisp and the cheese has melted. Cut into wedges, then serve with guacamole.

2 Chicken Tortilla Parcels

Mix 250 g (8 oz) ready-cooked rice with 100 g (3½ oz) canned black beans, rinsed and drained. Divide the rice mixture between 4 large tortillas. Scatter over 2 shredded ready-cooked chicken breasts, 2 chopped tomatoes, 1 tablespoon chopped shallot, the grated rind and juice of ½ lime and some fresh coriander. Sprinkle with 50 g (2 oz) grated Cheddar cheese and top each with 1 tablespoon soured cream. Fold over the sides, then roll up the tortillas to form parcels. Cook in a dry nonstick frying pan for 3–5 minutes on each side.

3 Chicken Tortilla Rolls with Tomato

Sauce Mix 500 ml (17 fl oz) tomato pasta sauce with 1 tablespoon sweet chilli sauce, 1 teaspoon ground cumin and a pinch of ground cinnamon. Stir 100 ml (3½ fl oz) of the mixture with 4 ready-cooked chicken breasts, torn into shreds, and 2 ready-roasted red peppers, cut into strips. Divide the chicken mixture between 8 tortillas, then roll up and place them, seam side down, in a shallow ovenproof dish. Pour over the remaining tomato sauce and scatter with 50 g (2 oz) grated Cheddar cheese and 100 g (3½ oz) sliced mozzarella cheese. Place in a preheated oven, 200°C (400°F), Gas Mark 6, for 20–25 minutes until bubbling and heated through.

# 20 Steamed Soy Chicken with Mixed Mushrooms

Serves 4

4 small skinless chicken breast
fillets
200 g (7 oz) mixed mushrooms
5 tablespoons soy sauce
finely grated rind and juice of
½ lime
1 chilli, sliced
1 garlic clove, chopped
1 teaspoon finely grated fresh
root ginger
handful of chopped fresh
coriander, to garnish
boiled jasmine rice (optional),
to serve

• Set a large steamer over a saucepan of gently simmering water. Place the chicken and mushrooms in a shallow, heatproof dish that will fit inside the steamer. Mix together the remaining ingredients and spoon over the chicken.

• Place the dish in the steamer, cover and cook for 15 minutes until the chicken is just cooked through. Scatter with coriander and serve with jasmine rice, if liked.

10 Soy-Fried Noodles with Chicken and Oyster Mushrooms

Heat a wok until smoking hot. Add 2 tablespoons vegetable oil and 300 g (10 oz) thinly sliced chicken breast. Stir-fry for 5 minutes, then add 1 crushed garlic clove, 1 teaspoon finely grated fresh root ginger and 200 g (7 oz) oyster mushrooms. Cook for a further 2 minutes. Stir in 300 g (10 oz) ready-cooked egg noodles, 100 g (3½ oz) baby spinach leaves and 4 tablespoons soy sauce mixed with 1 tablespoon sweet chilli sauce. Heat through until piping hot and serve immediately.

30 Roasted Soy Chicken with Shiitake Mushrooms

Mix 4 tablespoons soy sauce with the finely grated rind of 1 lemon, a squeeze of lemon juice, 1 crushed garlic clove and 1 finely chopped red chilli. Marinate 4 skinless chicken breast fillets in the mixture for 5–10 minutes. Remove from the marinade and place in a shallow roasting tin. Dot with 25 g (1 oz) butter, cut into small cubes, then place in a preheated oven, 200°C (400°F), Gas Mark 6, for 15 minutes. Arrange 200 g (7 oz) whole shiitake mushrooms around the chicken and pour over the marinade. Return to the oven for a further 5 minutes until the chicken and mushrooms are cooked through. Serve with plain noodles or rice, if liked.

Balti Chicken and Peppers

Serves 4

2 tablespoons vegetable oil

400 g (13 oz) skinless chicken breast fillets, diced

1 onion, sliced

2 garlic cloves, chopped

1 tablespoon finely grated fresh root ginger

1 tablespoon ground coriander

1 teaspoon ground fenugreek

1 teaspoon garam masala

1 red pepper, cored, deseeded and sliced

1 green pepper, cored, deseeded and sliced

5 tomatoes, chopped

50 ml (2 fl oz) double cream

2 tablespoons lemon juice

handful of chopped fresh coriander, to garnish

chapattis, to serve

• Heat the oil in a wok or balti dish. Add the chicken and cook for 5 minutes until golden all over, then remove from the pan and set aside. Add the onion and cook for 5 minutes until softened. Stir in the garlic and ginger and cook for 1 minute, then add the spices and stir around the pan.

• Add the peppers and stir until well coated. Stir in the tomatoes and chicken and cook for a further 5–7 minutes until the chicken is cooked through. Add the cream and lemon juice and season to taste. Sprinkle with the coriander and serve with some warm chapattis.

 Chicken Pasta with Chilli Pepper Pesto

Place 2 ready-roasted red peppers in a food processor with 25 g (1 oz) toasted flaked almonds, 2 tablespoons mascarpone cheese, 1 teaspoon balsamic vinegar, a pinch of dried chilli flakes and a handful of chopped basil. Blend to form a paste. Cook 500 g (1 lb) fresh penne according to the pack instructions, then drain. Stir in the pesto and 2 ready-cooked chicken breasts, torn into strips. Sprinkle with grated Parmesan cheese.

 Spicy Chicken and Pepper Bake

Peel and thinly slice 500 g (1 lb) new potatoes. Toss with 4 boneless, skinless chicken thighs, cut into chunks, 1 thickly sliced onion, 2 cored, deseeded and quartered red peppers, 3 tablespoons vegetable oil and 2 teaspoons garam masala. Spread out on a large baking sheet and season to taste. Place in a preheated oven, 220°C (425°F), Gas Mark 7, and cook for 15 minutes. Give the baking sheet a good shake, add 150 g (5 oz) cherry tomatoes and sprinkle with 1 teaspoon smoked paprika and the finely grated rind of 1 lemon. Return to the oven for a further 10 minutes or until the chicken and potatoes are cooked through. Drizzle over some natural yogurt and scatter with chopped fresh coriander to serve.

Baked Chicken, Potatoes and Asparagus with Gremolata

Serves 4

500 g (1 lb) new potatoes, thinly sliced
3 tablespoons olive oil
4 chicken breast fillets
150 g (5 oz) asparagus, trimmed
1 garlic clove, finely chopped

For the gremolata

finely grated rind of 1 lemon
large handful of chopped parsley
salt and pepper

- Toss the potatoes with 2 tablespoons of the oil and place in a large, shallow roasting tin. Place in a preheated oven, 200°C (400°F), Gas Mark 6, for 5 minutes, then arrange the chicken breasts on top and drizzle over a little more oil. Season well and return to the oven for a further 10 minutes.

- Arrange the asparagus spears in the tin, pour over any remaining oil and return to the oven for a further 5 minutes until golden and cooked through.

- To make the gremolata, mix together the garlic, lemon rind and parsley. Scatter over the chicken and vegetables before serving.

1 **Spaghetti with Chicken and Asparagus in Creamy Gremolata Sauce** Cook 400 g (13 oz) quick-cook spaghetti in a large saucepan of lightly salted boiling water according to the pack instructions. Add 150 g (5 oz) asparagus tips 3 minutes before the end of cooking, then add 75 g (3 oz) frozen peas 1 minute before the end. Drain and return the pasta and vegetables to the pan. Add 2 ready-cooked chicken breasts, cut into bite-sized pieces, 5 tablespoons crème fraîche, 1 crushed garlic clove, the finely grated rind of 1 lemon, a squeeze of lemon juice and plenty of chopped parsley. Season to taste, heat through and serve.

3 **Chicken, Asparagus and Gremolata Frittata** Heat 2 tablespoons olive oil in a large, nonstick frying pan. Add 100 g (3½ oz) asparagus tips and 1 crushed garlic clove and cook for 5 minutes until tender. Mix 1 ready-cooked chicken breast, cut into bite-sized pieces, with 6 beaten eggs, the finely grated rind of 1 lemon and a handful of chopped parsley. Season to taste and pour into the pan, mix gently together, then cook over a low heat for 15 minutes or until the egg is cooked through.

Linguine with Creamy Chicken Carbonara

Serves 4

500 g (1 lb) fresh linguine pasta
2 ready-cooked chicken breasts, torn into strips
1 egg, lightly beaten
4 tablespoons crème fraîche
finely grated rind of ½ lemon, plus 1 tablespoon juice
25 g (1 oz) Parmesan cheese, grated
salt and pepper
handful of chopped chives, to garnish

- Cook the linguine in a large saucepan of lightly salted boiling water according to the pack instructions. Drain, reserving a little of the cooking water, and return the pasta to the pan.

- Add the chicken to the pan with the egg, crème fraîche, lemon rind and juice and half the Parmesan.

- Season to taste and stir together, adding a little of the cooking water to loosen if necessary. Divide between bowls and sprinkle with the remaining Parmesan and the chives. Serve immediately.

 Penne with Creamy Pan-Fried Chicken and Lardons Heat 1 tablespoon olive oil in a large, heavy-based saucepan. Add 50 g (2 oz) lardons and cook until golden. Remove from the pan and set aside. Add 4 chicken breast fillets to the pan and cook for 5 minutes on each side. Return the lardons to the pan along with 50 ml (2 fl oz) hot chicken stock and 50 ml (2 fl oz) double cream. Stir in 300 g (10 oz) fresh penne pasta and simmer for 3 minutes until the pasta is 'al dente' and the chicken is cooked through. Stir in 50 g (2 oz) frozen peas and 2 tablespoons lemon juice and heat through. Season to taste and serve sprinkled with chopped chives.

 Pasta Bake with Creamy Chicken and Leeks Heat 1 tablespoon olive oil in a flameproof frying pan. Add 1 thinly sliced leek for and cook for 3 minutes to soften. Add 300 g (10 oz) diced chicken breast and cook for a further 2 minutes. Stir in 325 g (11 oz) dried penne pasta and 750 ml (1¼ pints) hot chicken stock, bring to the boil, then reduce the heat and simmer for 10 minutes. Add 200 ml (7 fl oz) double cream and continue to cook for a few minutes until the pasta is 'al dente' and the chicken is cooked through. Season to taste. Mix 50 g (2 oz) dried breadcrumbs with 25 g (1 oz) grated Parmesan cheese and the finely grated rind of 1 lemon. Sprinkle over the pasta mixture and cook under a preheated hot grill for 5 minutes until bubbling and crisp.

Seared Duck and Figs with Watercress Salad

Serves 4

4 duck breast fillets
4 figs, halved
½ teaspoon ground cinnamon
1 tablespoon balsamic vinegar
1 teaspoon honey
finely grated rind and juice of
    ½ orange
100 g (3½ oz) watercress
1 chicory head, leaves separated
salt and pepper

- Use a sharp knife to score a criss-cross pattern on the skin of the duck and season to taste. Heat a large frying pan until hot, add the duck, skin side down, and cook for 7 minutes. Pour away the excess oil and turn the duck over. Arrange the figs in the pan and cook for a further 5–7 minutes until the duck is cooked through and the figs softened.

- Remove the duck from the pan and cut into thick slices. Tip away any excess fat, then add the cinnamon, vinegar, honey and orange rind and juice to the pan and swirl around.

- Divide the watercress and chicory between plates, place the figs and sliced duck on top, then spoon over the warm dressing and serve immediately.

 Smoked Duck, Orange and Fig Salad Cut 4 figs in half, drizzle with a little olive oil and 1 teaspoon balsamic vinegar, then cook under a preheated hot grill for 2 minutes on each side until lightly charred. Toss 150 g (5 oz) watercress with 1 tablespoon sherry vinegar and 3 tablespoons olive oil and divide between serving plates. Peel 1 orange and cut into segments, then arrange on the plates with the grilled figs and 100 g (3½ oz) sliced smoked duck breast.

 Duck with Spicy Fig Couscous Use a sharp knife to score a criss-cross pattern on the skin of 4 duck breast fillets and season to taste. Heat a large frying pan until hot, add the duck, skin side down, and cook for 7 minutes. Pour away the excess oil and turn the duck over. Cook for a further 5 minutes, adding 1 crushed garlic clove to the pan for the last minute of cooking. Remove the frying pan from the heat and remove the duck from the pan.

Add 250 g (8 oz) couscous, 300 ml (½ pint) hot chicken stock and 4 chopped soft dried figs to the pan, cover tightly and leave for 7 minutes or until the couscous has softened. Add the finely grated rind and juice of ½ orange, then fork through 1 finely chopped red chilli and a large handful of chopped mint. Serve the couscous with the duck, cut into thick slices.

30 Herb-Roasted Turkey Breast with Pancetta and Beans

Serves 4

handful of chopped rosemary
handful of chopped parsley
25 g (1 oz) butter, softened
800 g (1 lb 10 oz) turkey breast
  joint
6 garlic cloves
50 ml (2 fl oz) dry white wine
50 ml (2 fl oz) hot chicken stock
4 pancetta slices
2 x 400 g (13 oz) cans butter
  beans, rinsed and drained
handful of sun-blush tomatoes,
  roughly chopped
50 ml (2 fl oz) double cream
salt and pepper

- Mix together the rosemary, three-quarters of the parsley and the butter and smear over the turkey joint. Season to taste.

- Place in a roasting tin with the garlic cloves, pour the wine and stock into the tin and arrange the pancetta on top of the turkey. Place in a preheated oven, 220°C (425°F), Gas Mark 7, for 25 minutes.

- Put the beans, tomatoes and cream into the roasting tin, topping up with a little water if necessary. Season to taste, then return to the oven for a further 3–5 minutes or until the turkey is cooked through and the beans are warm.

- Cut the turkey into slices and arrange on plates with the crispy pancetta and the beans, sprinkled with the remaining parsley.

 10 Spaghetti with Turkey, Ham and Beans Cook 500 g (1 lb) fresh spaghetti in a large saucepan of lightly salted boiling water according to the pack instructions. Add 200 g (7 oz) canned cannellini beans, rinsed and drained, for the last minute of cooking. Drain and then return to the pan. Add 4 slices of ready-cooked turkey, cut into strips, 2 slices of ham, cut into strips, and a handful of chopped sun-blush tomatoes. Stir in 4 tablespoons crème fraîche and 50 g (2 oz) rocket, then grate over plenty of Parmesan cheese to serve.

 20 Turkey, Bacon and Bean Stew Mix 400 g (13 oz) minced turkey with 2 finely chopped spring onions, 1 finely chopped bacon rasher and 1 egg yolk and season well. Roll the mixture into small balls. Heat 1 tablespoon oil in a deep frying pan. Fry the balls for 5 minutes until golden all over. Stir in 1 crushed garlic clove, then add a 200 g (7 oz) can chopped tomatoes and simmer for 5–10 minutes until the turkey balls are cooked through. Stir in a 400 g (13 oz) can butter beans, rinsed and drained, and heat through. Season to taste and scatter with parsley to serve.

QuickCook
Fish

Recipes listed by cooking time

10

Rice with Salmon and Lemon Ponzu Dressing

Serves 4

400 g (13 oz) jasmine rice
1 litre (1¾ pints) water
4 salmon fillets
2.5 cm (1 inch) piece of fresh root
    ginger, cut into matchsticks
1 red chilli, sliced
4 lemon slices
75 g (3 oz) frozen shelled
    edamame beans
1 tablespoon lemon juice
4 tablespoons soy sauce
1 tablespoon mirin
salt
1 spring onion, sliced,
    to garnish

- Put the rice and measurement water in a large, heavy-based casserole dish. Add a little salt and bring to the boil, then reduce the heat and simmer, uncovered, for 7 minutes until most of the water has boiled away.

- Place the salmon on top, scatter over the ginger and chilli and arrange a lemon slice on each piece of fish. Cover and cook for a further 7 minutes until the fish is just cooked through.

- Scatter over the edamame beans and leave to steam for 1 minute until heated through. Mix together the lemon juice, soy sauce and mirin and pour over the fish, then serve scattered with the spring onion.

10 Soba Noodles with Salmon and Lime Ponzu Dressing Cook 200 g (7 oz) soba noodles according to the pack instructions. Drain, cool under cold running water if necessary and drain again. Mix 4 tablespoons soy sauce with 1 tablespoon mirin and a squeeze of lime juice and toss with the noodles. Cut ¼ cucumber into thin slices and add to the noodles with 2 flaked hot-smoked salmon fillets and 2 sliced spring onions. Sprinkle with sesame seeds to serve.

30 Rice Noodles with Salmon and Lemon Teriyaki Dressing In a small bowl, mix 3 tablespoons soy sauce with 2 tablespoons mirin and 2 teaspoons finely grated fresh root ginger. Drizzle the soy sauce mixture over 4 salmon fillets and leave to marinate for 15 minutes. Heat 1 tablespoon olive oil in a frying pan. Shake the excess marinade from the salmon and cook for 5–7 minutes until starting to flake, then remove from the pan and set aside. Heat another tablespoon oil and cook 1 sliced shallot for 3 minutes, then stir in 1 crushed garlic clove and 150 g (5 oz) mangetout. Cook for 2 minutes until softened. Add 300 g (10 oz) ready-cooked rice noodles, the salmon marinade, 1 teaspoon sugar and a splash of water. Stir-fry for 1 minute, then return the salmon to the pan with 4 tablespoons lemon juice and heat through.

ONE-FISH-GOA

Prawn and Pea Risotto

Serves 4

2 tablespoons olive oil
1 onion, finely chopped
300 g (10 oz) risotto rice
100 ml (3½ fl oz) dry white wine
1 litre (1¾ pints) hot fish or
  chicken stock
250 g (8 oz) cooked peeled
  prawns
125 g (4 oz) frozen peas
finely grated rind of 1 lemon
25 g (1 oz) butter
2 tablespoons lemon juice
salt and pepper
handful of chopped mint leaves,
  to garnish

- Heat the oil in a large, heavy-based saucepan. Add the onion and cook for 5 minutes until softened. Stir in the risotto rice, followed by the wine and bubble until reduced by half.

- Gradually add the stock, a ladleful at a time, stirring continuously and allowing each ladleful to be absorbed before adding the next. Continue to cook for about 15 minutes, or until the rice is tender.

- Stir in the prawns, peas, lemon rind and butter and season to taste. Cover and leave to rest for a few minutes, then add the lemon juice and serve sprinkled with the mint.

 Stir-Fried Rice with Prawns and Peas

Heat 1 tablespoon vegetable oil in a wok or large frying pan. Add 1 crushed garlic clove and 1 teaspoon finely grated fresh root ginger and cook for 1 minute, then crack 1 egg into the pan and stir around to scramble. Add 300 g (10 oz) ready-cooked rice, 200 g (7 oz) cooked peeled prawns, 100 g (3½ oz) frozen peas and 1–2 tablespoons soy sauce. Heat through and serve immediately.

 Prawn, Pea and Rice Soup

Heat 1 tablespoon olive oil in a large, heavy-based saucepan. Add 2 finely chopped shallots and 1 crushed garlic clove and cook for 3 minutes until softened. Add 2 litres (3½ pints) hot chicken stock and 100 g (3½ oz) long grain rice and simmer for 15 minutes. Stir in 200 g (7 oz) cooked peeled prawns and 50 g (2 oz) frozen broad beans. Cook for 1 minute, then add 50 g (2 oz) frozen peas, the finely grated rind of 1 lemon, ½ finely chopped red chilli and a handful of chopped mint and heat through. Serve in warmed bowls with 1 tablespoon crème fraîche in each.

30 Spanish Monkfish and Clam Stew

Serves 4

3 tablespoons olive oil
1 onion, chopped
1 garlic clove, sliced
1 red pepper, cored, deseeded
  and sliced
pinch of dried chilli flakes
1 rosemary sprig
1 bay leaf
100 ml (3½ fl oz) dry white wine
pinch of saffron threads
400 g (13 oz) can chopped
  tomatoes
75 g (3 oz) blanched almonds,
  toasted and ground
625 g (1¼ lb) monkfish, cut into
  bite-sized pieces
500 g (1 lb) clams, rinsed and
  drained
salt and pepper

- Heat the oil in a wide saucepan or flameproof casserole dish. Add the onion and cook for 5 minutes until softened. Add the garlic and red pepper and cook for a further 2 minutes, then stir in the chilli and herbs and pour in the wine.

- Bring to the boil, then reduce the heat and simmer for 2 minutes. Add the saffron and tomatoes and simmer for a further 10 minutes, then stir in the almonds.

- Add the monkfish to the stew and cook for 3 minutes. Add the clams, cover the pan with a tightly fitting lid and continue to cook for about 5 minutes until the clams have opened, discarding any that have not. Remove the herbs and season the stew to taste.

10 Monkfish with Clam and Tomato Sauce

Heat 2 tablespoons olive oil in a large frying pan. Add 500 g (1 lb) monkfish medallions and cook for 3 minutes on each side. Stir in 1 chopped garlic clove and cook for 30 seconds, then add a 200 g (7 oz) can baby clams, drained, and 100 g (3½ oz) halved cherry tomatoes. Cook for 2 minutes, season well, scatter with 25 g (1 oz) toasted flaked almonds and a handful of chopped parsley.

20 Monkfish, Clam and Tomato

Parcels Cut 4 large squares of foil. Divide 500 g (1 lb) monkfish, cut into medallions, between the parcels and top with 100 g (3½ oz) halved cherry tomatoes. Add 1 rosemary sprig and 3 clams, rinsed and drained, to each. Season with salt and pepper, fold the foil over and roll up the edges to create airtight parcels, leaving just a little gap. Mix 50 ml (2 fl oz) dry white wine with a

pinch of saffron threads, pour a little into each parcel and then fully seal, leaving enough space in the packages for air to circulate. Place on a baking sheet and cook in a preheated oven, 220°C (425°F), Gas Mark 7, for 15 minutes until the parcels have puffed up and the clams have opened. Discard any clams that have not opened. Serve with crusty bread.

ONE-FISH-MYO

3 Crispy Fish Pie

Serves 4

butter, for greasing
200 g (7 oz) frozen spinach
400 g (13 oz) skinless salmon
   fillet, cubed
250 g (8 oz) skinless smoked
   haddock fillet, cubed
4 eggs
100 ml (3½ fl oz) crème fraîche
2 tablespoons boiling water
50 g (2 oz) dried breadcrumbs
salt and pepper

- Lightly grease an ovenproof dish. Place the spinach in a sieve and pour over boiling water from the kettle until it has defrosted. Lay the spinach on a sheet of kitchen paper and squeeze to get rid of excess water.

- Arrange the spinach in the ovenproof dish and place the fish on top. Make 4 small holes between the fish pieces and crack an egg into each one.

- Mix the crème fraîche with the measurement water and season to taste. Pour over the fish, then scatter with the breadcrumbs. Place in a preheated oven, 200°C (400°F), Gas Mark 6, for 25 minutes or until golden and bubbling and the fish is cooked through.

 Crispy Fish Nuggets

Cut 400 g (13 oz) chunky skinless salmon fillet into small bite-sized pieces and toss with 3 tablespoons olive oil. Place 100 g (3½ oz) dried white breadcrumbs, the finely grated rind of 1 lemon, a handful of chopped parsley and a pinch of salt in a freezer bag. Add the salmon and shake until well coated, then arrange the pieces on a lightly greased baking sheet. Drizzle with another tablespoon oil, then cook under a preheated hot grill for 5 minutes. Turn over and cook for a further 2–3 minutes until golden and cooked through. Serve with a tomato salad.

 Fish Pots with Crispy Topping

Divide 250 g (8 oz) skinless smoked haddock fillet, cut into small pieces, between 4 ramekins. Stir together 75 ml (3 fl oz) crème fraîche, a handful of chopped chives and 2 tablespoons water, then stir into the fish. Place in a preheated oven, 180°C (350°F), Gas Mark 4, for 5–7 minutes. Crack an egg on top of each ramekin, top with a sprinkling of dried breadcrumbs and a drizzle of melted butter, then return to the oven for a further 10–12 minutes until the eggs are set. Serve with crusty bread.

 Steamed Lemon Dill Salmon and Potatoes

Serves 2

400 g (13 oz) new potatoes, sliced

2 salmon fillets

75 g (3 oz) French beans, topped and tailed

4 tablespoons crème fraîche

finely grated rind and juice of ½ lemon

handful of chopped dill

1 tablespoon capers, rinsed and drained

salt and pepper

- Set a large steamer over a saucepan of gently simmering water. Place the potatoes in a shallow, heatproof dish which will fit inside the steamer and season well. Cover and cook for 10 minutes.

- Place the salmon on top of the potatoes and scatter around the beans. Cook for a further 7–10 minutes or until the fish and vegetables are cooked through.

- Meanwhile, mix together the crème fraîche, lemon rind and juice, dill and capers and season to taste. Serve with the salmon and vegetables.

 Salmon with Creamy Lemon Dill Beans Heat 1 tablespoon olive oil in a frying pan. Add 2 salmon fillets, skin side down, and cook for 5 minutes. Turn over and cook for a further 1 minute. Add 200 g (7 oz) canned cannellini beans, rinsed and drained, to the pan with 50 ml (2 fl oz) hot chicken stock and 3 tablespoons crème fraîche. Season to taste, heat through, then stir in the finely grated rind of 1 lemon and a handful of chopped dill. Serve with crusty bread.

Roasted Salmon, Potatoes and Asparagus with Lemon Dill Dressing Toss 2 tablespoons olive oil with 400 g (13 oz) potatoes, cut into cubes. Place in a shallow roasting tin and cook in a preheated oven, 200°C (400°F), Gas Mark 6, for 15 minutes, stirring halfway through cooking. Arrange 2 salmon fillets and 75 g (3 oz) asparagus spears in the tin, season to taste and return to the oven for a further 12–15 minutes until cooked through. Mix 2 tablespoons olive oil with the finely grated rind and juice of ½ lemon and a handful of chopped dill, season to taste and drizzle over the salmon and vegetables before serving.

Chilli Prawn Noodles

Serves 4

5 tablespoons tomato ketchup
2 tablespoons light soy sauce
2 teaspoons sugar
2 teaspoons cornflour
150 ml (¼ pint) water
2 tablespoons vegetable oil
1 red pepper, deseeded and sliced
2 garlic cloves, crushed
2 teaspoons finely grated fresh
   root ginger
1–2 red chillies, finely chopped
250 g (8 oz) cooked peeled
   prawns
300 g (10 oz) ready-cooked
   egg noodles
1 lime
2 spring onions, sliced

- Stir together the ketchup, soy sauce, sugar, cornflour and measurement water until smooth, then set aside. Heat a large wok or frying pan. Add the oil and swirl around the pan, then add the red pepper and cook for 2 minutes.

- Stir in the garlic, ginger and chilli and stir-fry for 1 minute, then add the prawns and the ketchup mixture and cook for 3 minutes until thickened.

- Add the noodles to the pan and cook until heated through and coated with the sauce. Squeeze over the lime juice, scatter with the spring onions and serve immediately.

 Chilli Prawn and Lime Couscous

Cook 1 finely chopped onion in 2 tablespoons oil for 5 minutes, then stir in 1 crushed garlic clove, 1 teaspoon chopped fresh root ginger, 1 chopped red chilli and ½ teaspoon ground cumin. Cook for 1 minute, then stir in 250 g (8 oz) raw peeled prawns and cook for 2 minutes. Remove from the heat, add 300 g (10 oz) couscous and 325 ml (11 fl oz) hot fish stock, cover and leave for 5 minutes. Add some chopped coriander, 1 sliced spring onion and the finely grated rind and juice of 1 lime, then fork through the couscous.

Chilli Prawn Bisque

Remove the shells from 500 g (1 lb) raw large prawns and chop the shells into small pieces. Heat 2 tablespoons vegetable oil in a large saucepan and cook the shells with 1 chopped onion until the onion is soft. Add 1 teaspoon tomato purée, 1–2 chopped red chillies, 2 chopped garlic cloves, a 2.5 cm (1 inch) piece of fresh root ginger and 1 lemon grass stalk and cook for 1 minute, then add 3 chopped tomatoes, 1.5 litres (2½ pints) hot fish or chicken stock and 50 g (2 oz) rice. Bring to the boil, then reduce the heat and simmer for 15–20 minutes until the rice is cooked. Remove the lemon grass and ginger, then pour the soup into a blender and whizz until smooth. Pass through a sieve back into the pan. Add the prawns, 100 ml (3½ fl oz) coconut cream and 1 tablespoon Thai fish sauce and cook for 3 minutes until the prawns are cooked through. Sprinkle with chopped fresh coriander to serve.

Spicy Fish and Potato Soup

Serves 4

1 tablespoon olive oil

2 garlic cloves, chopped

½ teaspoon ground cumin

½ teaspoon dried chilli flakes

1.2 litres (2 pints) hot fish or chicken stock

500 g (1 lb) small new potatoes, halved if large

3 tomatoes, chopped

400 g (13 oz) skinless firm white fish fillets, cut into pieces

1 tablespoon lemon juice

salt and pepper

To garnish

handful of chopped mint

handful of chopped coriander

- Heat the oil in a large, heavy-based saucepan. Add the garlic and cook for 30 seconds, then stir in the spices and stock and season to taste. Add the potatoes and bring to the boil, then reduce the heat and simmer for 12 minutes.

- Add the tomatoes and fish and cook for about 5 minutes until cooked through. Add the lemon juice, taste and adjust the seasoning if necessary. Ladle the soup into bowls and serve scattered with the herbs.

---

1 Spicy Grilled Fish with Chickpea Salad

Mix 1 teaspoon ground cumin with a pinch of dried chilli flakes, a pinch of salt and 1 tablespoon olive oil. Spread over 4 thin white fish fillets arranged on a baking sheet. Cook under a preheated hot grill for 7–9 minutes or until cooked through. Toss together a 400 g (13 oz) can chickpeas, rinsed and drained, 50 g (2 oz) sun-blush tomatoes, the finely grated rind of 1 lemon and a squeeze of lemon juice. Season to taste and serve with the fish and its juices, sprinkled with chopped fresh coriander.

3 Fish and Potato Bake with Spicy Herb Dressing Toss 750 g (1½ lb) new potatoes, halved if large, with 2 tablespoons olive oil and ½ teaspoon ground cumin. Place in a roasting tin and cook in a preheated oven, 220°C (425°F), Gas Mark 7, for 15 minutes. Add 4 white fish fillets and 100 g (3½ oz) cherry tomatoes, season to taste, then return to the oven for a further 10–15 minutes until the fish is cooked through. Meanwhile, place a large bunch of fresh coriander in a food processor with 1 chopped red chilli, 1 teaspoon ground cumin, 3 ground cardamom pods and 5 tablespoons olive oil and whizz together to make a dressing. Drizzle over the vegetables and fish before serving.

30 Baked Bacon-Wrapped Trout with Horseradish Sauce

Serves 4

750 g (1½ lb) potatoes, thinly
   sliced
3 tablespoons olive oil
4 small whole trout, gutted and
   scaled
1 lemon, sliced
4 thyme sprigs, plus extra
   to serve
4 thin bacon rashers
1 tablespoon horseradish sauce
200 g (7 oz) crème fraîche
salt and pepper

- Toss the potatoes with the oil, season to taste and place in a shallow roasting tin. Place in a preheated oven, 220°C (425°F), Gas Mark 7 for 15 minutes until starting to turn golden.

- Meanwhile, stuff the cavity of each trout with 2 lemon slices and a thyme sprig. Wrap 1 bacon rasher around each one, then arrange in the roasting tin. Return to the oven for a further 12–15 minutes until the fish and potatoes are cooked through.

- Meanwhile, mix the horseradish sauce with the crème fraiche. Serve with the potatoes and fish, scattered with some thyme.

---

10 Smoked Trout and Bacon Salad with Horseradish Dressing Cook 4 bacon rashers under a preheated hot grill for about 7 minutes until crisp, then break into pieces. Mix 2 teaspoons horseradish sauce with 100 ml (3½ fl oz) double cream and add lemon juice to taste. Place 200 g (7 oz) mixed rocket, watercress and spinach salad in a bowl with ½ sliced cucumber. Arrange 2 flaked smoked trout fillets on top, scatter over the bacon, then drizzle over the dressing.

20 Bacon-Wrapped Trout with Crispy Crumbs and Horseradish Cream Wrap 1 bacon rasher and a rosemary sprig around each of 4 small gutted and scaled trout. Arrange in a shallow roasting tin with 1 lemon, cut into wedges. Drizzle with 1 tablespoon olive oil and cook in a preheated oven, 200°C (400°F), Gas Mark 6, for 7 minutes. Tear 4 thick slices of white bread into chunks and scatter around the fish. Return to the oven for a further 7 minutes or until the fish is cooked through. Scatter with 25 g (1 oz) toasted flaked almonds. Whip 100 ml (3½ fl oz) double cream until soft peaks form, then stir in 1 tablespoon horseradish sauce and a little finely grated lemon rind. Serve the fish with the crispy crumbs, a handful of rocket leaves and the horseradish cream.

2 Clam, Kale and Butter Bean Stew

Serves 4

1 tablespoon olive oil
50 g (2 oz) chorizo, chopped
1 onion, finely chopped
2 garlic cloves, chopped
1 teaspoon tomato purée
50 ml (2 fl oz) dry white wine
200 ml (7 fl oz) hot chicken stock
75 g (3 oz) kale, chopped
500 g (1 lb) clams, rinsed and
  drained
200 g (7 oz) canned butter beans,
  rinsed and drained
salt and pepper

- Heat the oil in a large saucepan or flameproof casserole dish. Add the chorizo and cook for 1 minute until starting to release its oil. Add the onion and cook for a further 5 minutes until softened, then stir in the garlic and tomato purée and cook for 1 minute.

- Pour in the wine and let it bubble away until reduced by half. Add the stock and kale and cook for 5 minutes.

- Add the clams, cover and cook for 3 minutes, then stir in the beans. Cover and cook for a further 3 minutes until the clams have opened, discarding any that have not. Season to taste and serve.

---

1 **Stir-Fried Clams and Kale in Black Bean Sauce** Heat 2 tablespoons oil in a wok. Add 2 sliced garlic cloves and cook for a few seconds, then add 150 g (5 oz) chopped kale and stir-fry for 1–2 minutes. Add ½ finely chopped chilli and 2 teaspoons finely grated fresh root ginger and stir in, then add 500 g (1 lb) clams, rinsed and drained, and 75 ml (3 fl oz) black bean sauce. Add a splash of water, cover and cook for 5 minutes until the clams have opened, discarding any that have not. Scatter with 1 sliced spring onion before serving with plain rice, if liked.

3 **Clam, Lemon and Spinach Risotto** Heat 2 tablespoons olive oil in a large, heavy-based saucepan. Add 1 finely chopped onion and cook for 5 minutes until softened, then add 2 crushed garlic cloves and cook for a further 30 seconds. Stir in 300 g (10 oz) risotto rice, followed by 125 ml (4 fl oz) dry white wine and bubble until boiled away. Gradually add 1 litre (1¾ pints) hot chicken stock, a ladleful at a time, stirring continuously and allowing each ladleful to be absorbed before adding the next. After 10 minutes, add 400 g (13 oz) clams, rinsed and drained, and cook for a further 5 minutes until the rice is tender and the clams have opened, discarding any that have not. Add the finely grated rind of ½ lemon, 75 g (3 oz) baby spinach leaves and 75 g (3 oz) mascarpone cheese, then heat through and serve.

20 Spicy Salmon with Couscous

Serves 4

1 tablespoon olive oil, plus extra
  for greasing
1 teaspoon ground cumin
½ teaspoon ground coriander
pinch of dried chilli flakes
finely grated rind of 1 lemon
4 skinless salmon fillets
2 teaspoons runny honey
300 g (10 oz) couscous
325 ml (11 fl oz) hot chicken
  or fish stock
2 spring onions, sliced
25 g (1 oz) toasted flaked almonds
handful of chopped fresh
  coriander
salt and pepper

- Lightly grease a small roasting tin. Mix together the oil, spices and lemon rind and rub all over the salmon, season to taste and arrange in the roasting tin.

- Place in a preheated oven, 200°C (400°F), Gas Mark 6, for 10 minutes, drizzle over the honey and return to the oven for a further 3 minutes until golden and cooked through.

- Remove from the oven, scatter the couscous around the salmon and pour in the stock. Cover tightly with foil and leave for 5 minutes until the couscous is tender.

- Transfer the salmon to plates. Stir the spring onions, almonds and coriander into the couscous and serve with the salmon.

 Hot-Smoked Salmon Couscous Tabbouleh Tip 300 g (10 oz) couscous into a bowl and pour over 325 ml (11 fl oz) hot chicken stock. Cover and leave for 5 minutes until the couscous is soft. Mix the finely grated rind and juice of ½ lemon with ½ teaspoon ground cumin and 3 tablespoons olive oil, season to taste and stir through the couscous, fluffing it up. Add ¼ cucumber, finely chopped, 2 chopped tomatoes, 1 sliced spring onion, a large handful of chopped parsley and 250 g (8 oz) hot-smoked salmon, toss together and serve.

 Couscous-Crusted Salmon Tip 150 g (5 oz) couscous into a bowl and pour over 175 ml (6 fl oz) hot chicken stock. Cover and leave for 5 minutes until the couscous is tender. Add 25 g (1 oz) chopped pitted black olives, the finely grated rind of 1 orange and a handful of chopped parsley, season to taste and stir to fluff up. Brush 4 large skinless salmon fillets with 2 tablespoons olive oil, then dip the fillets in the couscous until well coated. Place on a greased baking sheet and cook in a preheated oven, 200°C (400°F), Gas Mark 6, for 12–15 minutes until the salmon is cooked through. Serve with green salad.

ONE-FISH-HAI

30 Smoked Haddock Kedgeree

Serves 4

1 tablespoon vegetable oil
25 g (1 oz) butter
1 onion, finely chopped
1 garlic clove, crushed
1 teaspoon finely grated fresh
  root ginger
1 teaspoon cumin seeds
½ teaspoon coriander seeds
1 teaspoon curry powder
½ teaspoon ground turmeric
300 g (10 oz) basmati rice
650 ml (1 pint 2 fl oz) hot chicken
  or fish stock
300 g (10 oz) skinless smoked
  haddock fillet
75 g (3 oz) frozen peas
1 red chilli, chopped
handful of chopped fresh coriander
salt and pepper
mango chutney, to serve

- Heat the oil and butter in a large saucepan. Add the onion and cook for 5 minutes, then stir in the garlic and ginger and cook for 1 minute. Add the cumin and coriander seeds and cook for 30 seconds, then stir in the curry powder, turmeric and rice and cook for a further 1 minute.

- Pour in the stock and cook for 5 minutes. Place the fish fillet on top of the rice and cook for a further 5 minutes. By this time, most of the stock should have boiled away. Add the peas, cover the pan tightly with a lid, turn down the heat as low as it will go and cook for 5–7 minutes until the rice is cooked through.

- Use a fork to gently break up the fish, stir the fish and peas into the rice and season to taste with salt and pepper. Scatter with the chilli and coriander and serve with mango chutney.

 Smoked Haddock in Creamy Curry Sauce Heat 1 tablespoon vegetable oil in a deep frying pan. Add 1 finely chopped shallot and cook for 2 minutes until softened. Stir in 1 teaspoon curry powder, then arrange 4 smoked haddock fillets in the pan. Cook for 1 minute, then pour in a splash of white wine and 100 ml (3½ fl oz) hot fish or chicken stock. Bring to the boil, then cover the pan and simmer for 5 minutes until the fish is cooked through. Stir in 2 tablespoons crème fraîche, then arrange the fish on plates and spoon the sauce on top. Serve with boiled rice, if liked.

2 Smoked Haddock, Rice and Spinach Soup Cook 1 chopped onion in 1 tablespoon oil for 5 minutes, then add 100 g (3½ oz) basmati rice, 1.5 litres (2½ pints) hot chicken or fish stock and a pinch of saffron threads. Simmer for 10 minutes, then add 300 g (10 oz) skinless smoked haddock fillet and cook for 3 minutes until starting to break up. Add 100 ml (3½ fl oz) single cream and 100 g (3½ oz) baby spinach leaves and heat through until wilted.

ONE-FISH-LAW

Thai Hot and Sour Prawn Soup

Serves 4

1 tablespoon tom yum or Thai red curry paste

1.5 litres (2½ pints) hot chicken or fish stock

2 cm (¾ inch) piece of fresh root ginger

1 lemon grass stalk

2 kaffir lime leaves

1 teaspoon brown sugar

1 tablespoon Thai fish sauce

400 g (13 oz) oyster mushrooms, sliced

250 g (8 oz) raw large prawns

lime juice, to taste

handful of chopped fresh coriander, to garnish

- Heat a large, heavy-based saucepan. Add the curry paste, then stir in the stock, ginger, lemon grass, lime leaves, sugar and fish sauce. Bring to the boil, then reduce the heat and simmer for 5 minutes.

- Add the mushrooms and prawns and season to taste. Cook for a further 3–4 minutes until the prawns are just cooked through. Add lime juice to taste, remove the ginger, lemon grass and lime leaves if liked, and serve immediately, scattered with the coriander.

 Thai Spicy Prawn Soup with Sweet Potato Heat 1 tablespoon vegetable oil in a large, heavy-based saucepan. Add 1 tablespoon Thai red curry paste and cook for 1 minute, then add 1.5 litres (2½ pints) hot chicken stock and bring to the boil. Add a 2 cm (¾ inch) piece of fresh root ginger, 1 kaffir lime leaf and 1 lemon grass stalk and simmer for 5 minutes. Add 1 large sweet potato, peeled and cubed, and cook for 7–10 minutes until tender. Add 250 g (8 oz) cooked large prawns and heat through. Serve scattered with 1 chopped red chilli and coriander leaves.

 Thai Hot and Sour Prawn Jungle Curry Place 2 tablespoons chopped fresh root ginger, 1 crushed garlic clove, 1 chopped green chilli, 1 chopped lemon grass stalk, 1 small shallot and a handful of fresh coriander in a small food processor and blend to a smooth paste. Peel 250 g (8 oz) raw large prawns. Heat 2 tablespoons vegetable oil in a large saucepan, add the prawn shells and cook for 5 minutes, crushing as you go, until golden. Add the paste and cook for 2 minutes until fragrant. Add 2 tablespoons Thai fish sauce, 200 ml (7 fl oz) hot vegetable or chicken stock and 2 kaffir lime leaves and simmer for 10 minutes. Strain the liquid, return to the pan and add 1 chopped aubergine. Cook for 5 minutes to soften, then add the prawns, 150 g (5 oz) snake beans or French beans and 100 g (3½ oz) cooked bamboo shoots. Cook for 3–5 minutes until the prawns are cooked through. Scatter with chopped fresh coriander to serve.

30 Baked Tuna with Ratatouille

Serves 4

1 onion, cut into wedges
1 aubergine, cut into chunks
1 red pepper, cored, deseeded
   and cut into chunks
1 courgette, thickly sliced
4 tomatoes, quartered
5 tablespoons olive oil
2 garlic cloves, crushed
1 tablespoon sherry vinegar
4 tuna steaks
salt and pepper
handful of chopped basil,
   to garnish

- Toss the vegetables with 3 tablespoons of the oil, arrange in a shallow roasting dish and season to taste. Place in a preheated oven, 200°C (400°F), Gas Mark 6, for 15 minutes, turning occasionally, until lightly charred.

- Mix the remaining oil with the garlic and vinegar and stir into the vegetables. Arrange the tuna steaks in the dish and season well. Return to the oven for a further 12–15 minutes until the tuna is cooked. Serve immediately, scattered with the basil.

1 Seared Tuna with Ratatouille Salad

Rub 1 tablespoon olive oil over 4 tuna steaks and season to taste. Cook in a preheated hot griddle pan for 2–3 minutes on each side until golden on the outside but still pink in the middle. Set aside. Mix together 2 teaspoons balsamic vinegar, 3 tablespoons olive oil and 1 crushed garlic clove. Season to taste. Toss with 150 g (5 oz) rocket, 1 ready-roasted red pepper, 1 ready-roasted aubergine, cut into strips, and 100 g (3½ oz) halved cherry tomatoes. Serve the salad with the tuna.

2 Roasted Tuna with Ratatouille

Topping Rub 1 tablespoon olive oil over 4 tuna steaks and place in a shallow roasting tin. Scatter 75 g (3 oz) halved cherry tomatoes, 1 cored, deseeded and chopped red pepper, 1 sliced garlic clove and 1 tablespoon capers, rinsed and drained, over the fish, season well and drizzle over another tablespoon oil. Place in a preheated oven, 200°C (400°F), Gas Mark 6, for 12–15 minutes until the vegetables are lightly charred and the tuna is cooked. Sprinkle with chopped basil before serving with crusty bread.

ONE-FISH-ZOF

20 Baked Cod Parcels with Beans and Chorizo

Serves 4

4 cod fillets

400 g (13 oz) canned butter beans, rinsed and drained

125 g (4 oz) cherry tomatoes, halved

4 thyme sprigs

4 thin chorizo slices

75 ml (3 fl oz) dry white wine

salt and pepper

- Cut 4 large sheets of baking paper and place a cod fillet on each. Divide the beans, tomatoes and thyme between the parcels and season well.

- Place a chorizo slice on top of each piece of fish and season with salt and pepper, then fold the paper over and roll up the edges to create airtight parcels, leaving just a little gap.

- Pour a little wine into each parcel and then fully seal, leaving enough space in the packages for air to circulate. Place on a baking sheet and cook in a preheated oven, 220°C (425°F), Gas Mark 7, for 15 minutes until the fish is cooked through.

10 Seared Cod with Bean and Tomato

Salad Rub 1 tablespoon olive oil over 4 cod fillets and season well. Place skin side down in a preheated griddle pan and cook for 5 minutes. Turn over and cook for a further 3 minutes until golden and cooked through. Meanwhile, whisk together 1 tablespoon balsamic vinegar and 3 tablespoons olive oil. Add 250 g (8 oz) halved cherry tomatoes and a 400 g (13 oz) can butter beans, rinsed and drained. Season to taste and add 100 g (3½ oz) rocket and ½ chopped red chilli. Serve the salad with the cod.

30 Spicy Cod and Bean Stew

Heat 2 tablespoons olive oil in a flameproof casserole dish. Add 3 chopped bacon rashers and cook for 2 minutes until golden, then add 1 chopped onion and cook for 5 minutes until softened. Stir in 2 crushed garlic cloves and 1 teaspoon smoked paprika. Pour in 75 ml (3 fl oz) dry white wine and cook for a further 3 minutes. Add 200 g (7 oz) chopped tomatoes and 2 thyme sprigs and simmer for 5 minutes. Season well, then add 200 g (7 oz) canned butter beans, rinsed and drained, and heat through. Slide 4 cod fillets into the stew, cover tightly and cook for 12–15 minutes until the fish is cooked through. Scatter with chopped parsley before serving.

ONE-FISH-BUJ

1 Seabass with Herb and Olive Israeli Couscous

Serves 4

50 ml (2 fl oz) dry white wine
300 g (10 oz) Israeli couscous
350 ml (12 fl oz) hot vegetable stock
4 seabass fillets
2 tablespoons extra virgin olive oil
50 g (2 oz) pitted black olives
1 ready-roasted red pepper, sliced
handful of chopped basil
handful of chopped parsley
salt and pepper

- Pour the wine into a shallow flameproof casserole dish and boil for 1 minute. Add the couscous and stock and stir well, then arrange the fish on top. Cover and leave to cook gently for 8 minutes until the fish and couscous are cooked through.

- Transfer the fish to warmed plates, stir the remaining ingredients into the couscous, season to taste and serve with the fish.

2 Charred Pepper and Seabass Bake

with Israeli Couscous Cut a red pepper into wedges and arrange in a shallow roasting tin with 4 seabass fillets and 3 garlic cloves. Rub 2 tablespoons olive oil over the ingredients in the tin, season to taste and place in a preheated oven, 220°C (425°F), Gas Mark 7, for 10 minutes. Add 300 g (10 oz) Israeli couscous and 350 ml (12 fl oz) hot vegetable stock to the tin. Cover with foil and return to the oven for a further 5 minutes. Leave to steam, covered, for a few more minutes until cooked through. Stir in 4 tablespoons lemon juice, 1 sliced spring onion and a handful of chopped basil and serve immediately.

3 Spicy Seabass and Israeli Couscous

Stew Heat 2 tablespoons olive oil in a large, heavy-based saucepan. Add 1 chopped onion and cook for 5 minutes until softened. Stir in 1 crushed garlic clove and cook for 30 seconds. Add 1 teaspoon ground cumin, 1 cinnamon stick, a 200 g (7 oz) can chopped tomatoes and 500 ml (17 fl oz) hot vegetable stock. Season to taste, add a pinch of saffron threads and simmer for 10 minutes. Add 1 sliced red pepper and 200 g (7 oz) Israeli couscous and cook for 3 minutes. Add 4 seabass fillets, cut into bite-sized pieces, and continue to cook for about 5 minutes until cooked through. Scatter with parsley to serve.

Fish, Coconut and Potato Curry

Serves 4

2 tablespoons vegetable oil
1 teaspoon mustard seeds
½ teaspoon fenugreek seeds
1 onion, sliced
2 garlic cloves, finely chopped
1 tablespoon finely grated fresh
  root ginger
1 green chilli, chopped
1 teaspoon ground turmeric
1 teaspoon ground coriander
1 stalk of curry leaves
1 tablespoon tamarind paste
400 ml (14 fl oz) coconut milk
400 g (13 oz) new potatoes,
  halved
150 g (5 oz) cherry tomatoes,
  halved
400 g (13 oz) skinless cod or
  haddock fillet, cut into chunks

- Heat the oil in a large saucepan. Add the mustard and fenugreek seeds and cook for 30 seconds until they sizzle. Add the onion and cook for 3–4 minutes until softened.

- Stir in the garlic, ginger and chilli, followed by the ground spices and curry leaves and cook for 1 minute. Add the tamarind and coconut milk, season to taste and bring to the boil.

- Add the potatoes and cook for 7 minutes, then add the tomatoes and fish and simmer for a further 7 minutes until the fish and potatoes are cooked through.

Fish and Coconut Tikka

Mix 3 tablespoons coconut cream with 1 tablespoon tikka curry paste. Stir in 400 g (13 oz) skinless cod fillet, cut into thick chunks. Thread the fish on to metal skewers, alternating with whole cherry tomatoes. Drizzle over a little vegetable oil, and cook under a preheated hot grill for 4 minutes on each side until cooked through. Serve wrapped in chapattis with some green salad and desiccated coconut.

Spicy Fish, Coconut and Potato Bake

Place 2 crushed garlic cloves, 2 teaspoons finely grated fresh root ginger, 1 chopped red chilli, 1 teaspoon ground cumin, 1 teaspoon ground coriander, a pinch of turmeric, 1 tablespoon vegetable oil and 4 tablespoons coconut cream in a food processor and blend until smooth. Season. Make 3 slashes across each side of a whole gutted and scaled 1.25 kg (2½ lb) seabass. Rub the paste over the fish and place 2 lemon slices inside the cavity. Place in a lightly oiled roasting tin with 500 g (1 lb) new potatoes, thinly sliced. Pour in 125 ml (4 fl oz) water, cover with foil and place in a preheated oven, 200°C (400°F), Gas Mark 6, for 15 minutes. Remove the foil and arrange 5 large tomatoes, quartered, around the fish. Return to the oven for 10 minutes until the fish and potatoes are cooked through. Serve sprinkled with coriander leaves.

30 Baked Pancetta-Wrapped Monkfish with Tapenade

Serves 4

750 g (1½ lb) new potatoes
2 tablespoons olive oil
15 pancetta slices
400 g (13 oz) monkfish, boned
 and cut into 4 fillets
1 red pepper, cored, deseeded and
 cut into chunks
handful of chopped parsley
4 tablespoons tapenade
salt and pepper

- Toss the potatoes with the oil, season to taste and place in a large, shallow roasting tin. Place in a preheated oven, 220°C (425°F), Gas Mark 7 for 5 minutes.

- Meanwhile, lay the pancetta slices on a large piece of greaseproof paper so they are slightly overlapping. Season the monkfish fillets and place side by side on the pancetta, with one thick end and one thin end at each side to make a uniform shape. Use the greaseproof paper to help you lift the pancetta up and over the fish so it is tightly wrapped.

- Give the potatoes a good shake, then add the monkfish and red pepper to the tin. Return to the oven for a further 15–20 minutes until the fish and potatoes are cooked through. Meanwhile, stir the parsley into the tapenade, then serve with the fish and vegetables.

 Pancetta-Wrapped Monkfish Skewers

Cut 400 g (13 oz) monkfish tail into bite-sized pieces and wrap half a slice of pancetta around each one. Thread on to metal skewers, alternating with chunks of red pepper and leaving a little space at the end. Drizzle with 1 tablespoon olive oil and cook under a preheated hot grill for 2 minutes. Thread ¼ baguette, cut into chunks, on to the ends of the skewers, drizzle with a little more oil and cook for 5 minutes, turning occasionally, until the fish is cooked through. Serve with a herby green salad tossed with 50 g (2 oz) pitted black olives.

 Baked Pancetta-Wrapped Monkfish Cutlets Cut 400 g (13 oz) monkfish tail into 2 cm (¾ inch) slices. Wrap a slice of pancetta around each piece of fish and arrange close together in a roasting tin, tucking slices of red pepper between them. Chop 3 tomatoes and mix with 50 g (2 oz) roughly chopped black olives, 1 crushed garlic clove, the finely grated rind of 1 lemon and 3 tablespoons olive oil. Scatter over the fish, season to taste and cook in a preheated oven, 220°C (425°F), Gas Mark 7, for 15 minutes until cooked through. Serve with crusty bread.

30 Smoked Haddock and Watercress Cannelloni

Serves 4

butter, for greasing
400 g (13 oz) skinless smoked
   haddock fillet, cut into pieces
300 ml (½ pint) boiling water
300 g (10 oz) watercress
200 ml (7 fl oz) crème fraîche
8 fresh lasagne sheets
50 g (2 oz) dried breadcrumbs
salt and pepper

- Lightly grease an ovenproof dish. Place the haddock in a bowl, pour over the measurement water and leave for 3 minutes. Drain, reserving the water, and break up the fish.

- Place the watercress in a colander and pour over boiling water from the kettle until it has wilted. Place on a sheet of kitchen paper and squeeze away excess water, then roughly chop. Mix with the haddock and 2 tablespoons of the crème fraîche.

- Divide the haddock mixture between the lasagne sheets, arranging it in strip down the middle. Roll up and arrange snugly, seam side down, in the ovenproof dish. Mix the remaining crème fraîche with the haddock soaking water, season and pour over the top.

- Scatter the breadcrumbs over the pasta, cover the dish with foil and place in a preheated oven, 200°C (400°F), Gas Mark 6, for 20 minutes. Remove the foil and cook under a preheated hot grill until the breadcrumbs are golden.

 Smoked Mackerel and Watercress Omelettes Lightly beat 5 eggs in a bowl and season to taste. Heat 1 teaspoon olive oil in a small nonstick frying pan, add one-quarter of the beaten egg and cook for 30 seconds, stirring a little with a spatula. Scatter with 25 g (1 oz) flaked smoked mackerel and cook for a further 30 seconds until just set. Scatter with a handful of chopped watercress, fold over and serve. Repeat with the remaining mixture to make 3 more omelettes.

 Smoked Haddock and Watercress Soup Heat 1 tablespoon olive oil in a large, heavy-based saucepan. Add 1 chopped onion and cook gently for 5 minutes, then add 1 finely diced potato, 750 ml (1¼ pints) vegetable stock and 2 smoked haddock fillets. Simmer for 7 minutes, then remove the haddock and flake into chunks. Cook the soup for a further 5 minutes until the potato is just soft, then add 200 g (7 oz) watercress and 50 ml (2 fl oz) double cream. Use a hand-held electric stick blender to purée the soup until smooth, season with pepper, then return the haddock to the soup and serve.

Seared Tuna with Lemon, Bean and Rocket Salad

Serves 4

1 tablespoon olive oil

4 tuna steaks

2–4 tablespoons lemon juice

finely grated rind of ½ lemon

3 tablespoons extra virgin olive oil

2 x 400 g (13 oz) cans cannellini beans, rinsed and drained

100 g (3½ oz) rocket

1 small red onion, finely sliced

1 red chilli, deseeded and chopped

salt and pepper

- Rub the olive oil over the tuna steaks and season well. Heat a griddle pan until smoking hot, then cook the tuna for 1–2 minutes on each side until charred on the outside but still pink in the middle.

- Meanwhile, mix 2 tablespoons of the lemon juice with the extra virgin olive oil and season to taste. Toss with the remaining ingredients and add more lemon juice if required. Serve the bean salad with the seared tuna.

Lemony Tuna, Bean and Rocket Bake

Mix 200 ml (7 fl oz) crème fraîche with 4 tablespoons boiling water and the finely grated rind of 1 lemon. Add 2 x 400 g (13 oz) cans cannellini beans, rinsed and drained, 200 g (7 oz) canned tuna, drained, and 50 g (2 oz) chopped rocket. Season to taste, place in an ovenproof dish and scatter with 75 g (3 oz) dried breadcrumbs mixed with 2 tablespoons finely grated Parmesan cheese. Place in a preheated oven, 200°C (400°F), Gas Mark 6, for 15 minutes until golden and bubbling.

Creamy Tuna and Bean Risotto with Lemon and Rocket

Heat 2 tablespoons olive oil in a large, heavy-based saucepan. Add 1 finely chopped onion and cook for 5 minutes until softened, then stir in 250 g (8 oz) risotto rice, followed by 50 ml (2 fl oz) dry white wine and bubble until boiled away. Gradually add 600 ml (1 pint) hot vegetable stock, a ladleful at a time, stirring continuously and allowing each ladleful to be absorbed before adding the next. After 15 minutes, add 200 g (7 oz) canned cannellini beans, rinsed and drained, and cook for a further 3–5 minutes until the rice is tender. Stir in 200 g (7 oz) canned tuna, drained, and 50 g (2 oz) finely grated Parmesan cheese. Season to taste, spoon into bowls and serve topped with the finely grated rind of ½ lemon and a handful of chopped rocket leaves.

30 Oven-Baked Fish and Chips with Tomato Salsa

Serves 4

750 g (1½ lb) potatoes, cut into thin wedges
4 tablespoons olive oil
4 skinless cod or haddock fillets
Finely grated rind of 1 lemon
1 teaspoon balsamic vinegar
4 tomatoes, chopped
1 teaspoon capers, rinsed and drained
1 spring onion, chopped
salt and pepper
handful of chopped parsley, to garnish

- Toss the potatoes with half the olive oil, season well and arrange in a shallow roasting tin. Place in a preheated oven, 220°C (425°F), Gas Mark 7, for 10 minutes.

- Turn over the potatoes, place the fish on top, season again and scatter over the lemon rind. Return to the oven for a further 15–20 minutes until the potatoes are just cooked through.

- Meanwhile, mix the remaining oil with the vinegar, season to taste and stir in the tomatoes, capers and spring onion. Serve the fish scattered with the parsley, with the chips and salsa on the side.

 Grilled Fish with Polenta Chips

Brush 3 tablespoons olive oil over 4 skinless cod fillets and 500 g (1 lb) ready-made polenta, cut into chips. Season to taste and cook under a preheated hot grill for 5 minutes. Turn the polenta chips over, scatter 125 g (4 oz) halved cherry tomatoes into the grill pan and cook for a further 3 minutes until the fish is cooked through. Sprinkle with chopped basil and serve immediately.

 Fish Fingers with Sweet Potato

Chips Toss 2 tablespoons olive oil with 750 g (1½ lb) sweet potatoes, peeled and cut into thin wedges. Season to taste, place in a shallow roasting tin and cook in a preheated oven, 200°C (400°F), Gas Mark 6, for 7 minutes. Meanwhile, brush 3 tablespoons mayonnaise over 400 g (13 oz) skinless cod fillet, cut into fingers. Finely grate the rind of 1 lemon and mix with 75 g (3 oz) dried breadcrumbs on a plate. Toss the fish in the crumbs until coated. Place in the roasting tin and return to the oven for a further 10 minutes until cooked through.

1 Prawn Salad with Peanut Sauce

Serves 4

200 g (7 oz) dried thin rice noodles

6 tablespoons crunchy peanut butter

1 tablespoon sweet chilli sauce

2 tablespoons soy sauce

4 tablespoons boiling water

200 g (7 oz) cooked peeled large prawns

½ iceberg lettuce, shredded

1 large carrot, cut into matchsticks

½ cucumber, cut into matchsticks

2 spring onions, shredded

- Soak the rice noodles according to the pack instructions. Mix the peanut butter with the chilli sauce, soy sauce and measurement water until smooth.

- Drain the noodles, cool under cold running water and drain again. Toss with the remaining ingredients, season with salt and pepper, then drizzle over the sauce to serve.

---

2 Egg-Fried Rice with Prawns and Peanuts

Heat a wok until smoking hot. Add 1 tablespoon vegetable oil and swirl around the pan. Add 2 beaten eggs, stir around for 2 minutes until set, then remove from the pan and set aside. Add another tablespoon oil to the pan, then add 200 g (7 oz) raw peeled large prawns. Cook for 3–5 minutes until pink, then remove from the pan and set aside. Heat another tablespoon oil, add 1 finely chopped shallot and cook for 2 minutes to soften. Stir in 1 crushed garlic clove and 2 teaspoons finely grated fresh root ginger. Cook for 1 minute, then add 250 g (8 oz) ready-cooked rice and 50 g (2 oz) bean sprouts. Stir around the pan, then add the egg and prawns. Mix together 2 tablespoons lime juice, 2 tablespoons peanut butter and 2 tablespoons soy sauce and pour into the pan. Stir well, then serve topped with chopped fresh coriander and a handful of chopped roasted peanuts.

3 Prawn and Peanut Curry

Heat 1 tablespoon vegetable oil in a casserole and add 1 tablespoon Thai red curry paste. Cook over a low heat for about 5 minutes until the oil starts to separate. Stir in 2 tablespoons peanut butter, then add 400 ml (14 fl oz) coconut milk and bring to the boil. Add 2 lime leaves, 1 lemon grass stalk, 1 tablespoon Thai fish sauce and 1 teaspoon sugar and simmer for 10 minutes. Add 1 sliced red pepper and cook for 2 minutes, then stir in 150 g (5 oz) baby sweetcorn and cook for a further 2 minutes. Add 200 g (7 oz) raw peeled large prawns and cook for 5 minutes until cooked through. Scatter with chopped fresh coriander.

ONE-FISH-PUF

Spicy Seafood Pasta with Garlic Mayonnaise

Serves 4

2 tablespoons olive oil

1 onion, finely chopped

3 garlic cloves, crushed

½ teaspoon fennel seeds

1 teaspoon smoked paprika

250 g (8 oz) angel hair pasta, broken into 3 cm (1¼ inch) lengths

400 g (13 oz) can chopped tomatoes

750 ml (1¼ pints) hot fish stock

150 g (5 oz) prepared squid, cut into rings

250 g (8 oz) mussels, scrubbed, rinsed and drained

100 g (3½ oz) raw peeled prawns

5 tablespoons mayonnaise

salt and pepper

handful of chopped parsley, to garnish

- Heat the oil in a large frying pan. Add the onion and cook for 5 minutes until soft, then add 2 of the garlic cloves and cook for a further 1 minute. Stir in the fennel seeds, paprika and pasta and stir for 1 minute until coated.

- Pour in the tomatoes and stock, season and bring to the boil. Simmer for 10 minutes, then add the squid, mussels and prawns and cook for 3–5 minutes until the seafood is cooked through, discarding any mussels that don't open.

- Meanwhile, mix the mayonnaise with the remaining garlic. Serve with the pasta, which has been scattered with the parsley.

 Quick Spicy Seafood Spaghetti

Cook 500 g (1 lb) fresh spaghetti according to the pack instructions, then drain and return to the saucepan. Add 1 small crushed garlic clove, 2 chopped tomatoes, 1 chopped chilli, 125 g (4 oz) cooked peeled prawns, 125 g (4 oz) cooked shelled mussels and 2 tablespoons olive oil. Squeeze over a little lemon juice, add a handful of chopped parsley, season to taste, then toss together and serve.

 Spanish Seafood Rice

Heat 2 tablespoons olive oil in a deep frying pan with a lid. Add 300 g (10 oz) monkfish, cut into thin slices, and cook for 2 minutes on each side until golden, then remove from the pan and set aside. Add 1 finely chopped onion to the pan and cook for 1 minute, then stir in 2 crushed garlic cloves. Add 2 teaspoons tomato purée and 300 g (10 oz) paella rice, stir well and add 750 ml (1¼ pints) hot fish stock and a pinch of saffron threads. Leave to simmer for 10 minutes, then add 300 g (10 oz) clams, rinsed and drained, and 150 g (5 oz) raw peeled prawns. Cover and steam for 5 minutes until the clams have opened, discarding any that have not. Return the monkfish to the pan and continue to cook for a few minutes until the rice and fish are cooked through. Serve with lemon wedges.

ONE-FISH-LYW

30 Cod with Creamy Chowder Sauce

Serves 4

1 tablespoon vegetable oil
4 smoked bacon rashers, chopped
1 tablespoon butter
2 leeks, sliced
1 tablespoon flour
750 ml (1¼ pints) fish stock
200 ml (7 fl oz) milk
400 g (13 oz) potatoes, diced
4 cod fillets
100 ml (3½ fl oz) double cream
salt and pepper
handful of chopped chives,
  to garnish

- Heat the oil in a large, heavy-based saucepan. Add the bacon and cook for 5 minutes until crisp, then remove from the pan and set aside. Add the butter and leeks to the pan and cook for 3–5 minutes until softened.

- Stir in the flour, then gradually add the stock and milk, stirring continuously to avoid any lumps forming. Bring to the boil, add the potatoes and simmer for 7 minutes.

- Arrange the cod fillets in the pan and cook for a further 7 minutes until they are cooked through. Transfer the cod to warmed shallow serving bowls.

- Stir the cream and most of the bacon into the sauce and season to taste. Warm through and ladle around the fish. Serve sprinkled with chives and the remaining bacon.

1 Smoked Cod with Cream and Spinach

Place 4 smoked cod fillets in a saucepan. Add 300 ml (½ pint) hot fish or vegetable stock, bring to the boil, reduce the heat and simmer for 5–7 minutes until the fish flakes. Remove the fish and keep warm. Meanwhile, mix 125 g (4 oz) crème fraîche with 1 egg yolk. Stir in 50 ml (2 fl oz) of the poaching liquid, then return to the pan and gently heat through until it thickens a little. Place 150 g (5 oz) spinach in a sieve and pour over boiling water until it has wilted. Arrange on warmed plates and top with the cod. Add a little lemon juice and pepper to the sauce and pour over the fish.

2 Creamy Smoked Cod and Sweetcorn

Chowder Heat 1 tablespoon each vegetable oil and butter in a pan. Add 1 finely chopped onion and cook for 5 minutes until softened. Add 1 litre (1¾ pints) fish or chicken stock and 200 ml (7 fl oz) milk and bring to the boil. Add 400 g (13 oz) new potatoes, halved, and simmer for 7 minutes, then add 300 g (10 oz) smoked cod fillets and cook for a further 5 minutes. Transfer the fish to a plate, remove any skin and bones and break it into large flakes. Return to the soup with 125 g (4 oz) frozen sweetcorn and 100 ml (3½ fl oz) double cream. Heat through, season with pepper and serve sprinkled with chopped parsley.

Rosti with Smoked Salmon and Rocket

Serves 4

750 g (1½ lb) waxy potatoes, coarsely grated

1 small onion, coarsely grated

50 g (2 oz) butter

3 tablespoons olive oil

2 tablespoons lemon juice

100 g (3½ oz) rocket

250 g (8 oz) smoked salmon

salt and pepper

lemon wedges, to serve

- Place the potatoes and onion in a clean tea towel and squeeze to remove excess moisture. Season well. Heat the butter and 1 tablespoon of the oil in a nonstick frying pan.

- Tip in the potato mixture and spread out to make an even layer, then cook for about 10 minutes until golden. Invert the rosti on to a plate, then carefully slide back into the pan the other way up to cook the other side. Cook for a further 5–8 minutes until cooked through and golden all over.

- Meanwhile, mix the lemon juice with the remaining oil and toss with the rocket. Cut the rosti into wedges and serve with slices of smoked salmon, the rocket salad and lemon wedges.

 Smoked Salmon and Rocket Pasta Cook 500 g (1 lb) fresh penne in a large saucepan of lightly salted boiling water according to the pack instructions. Drain and return to the pan. Add 4 tablespoons crème fraîche, 2 tablespoons lemon juice and 175 g (6 oz) smoked salmon, cut into strips. Toss through 75 g (3 oz) rocket and season to taste just before serving.

 Roast Salmon and Potatoes with Rocket Dressing Toss 750 g (1½ lb) halved new potatoes with 3 tablespoons olive oil and place in a roasting tin. Season to taste and cook in a preheated oven, 200°C (400°F), Gas Mark 6, for 15 minutes, turning once during cooking. Arrange 4 salmon fillets in the tin with the potatoes, season to taste, then return to the oven for a further 12–15 minutes until the fish and potatoes are cooked through. Meanwhile, mix 150 g (5 oz) chopped rocket with 1 tablespoon capers, rinsed and drained, the finely grated rind and juice of ½ lemon and 3 tablespoons olive oil. Spoon over the salmon and potatoes before serving.

QuickCook
Meat

Recipes listed by cooking time

30

20

10

30 Roasted Sausages with Parsnips and Carrots

Serves 4

8 pork sausages
1 onion, cut into wedges
2 large carrots, cut into wedges
2 large parsnips, cut into wedges
4 garlic cloves, unpeeled
2 tablespoons olive oil
1 teaspoon runny honey
handful of rosemary sprigs
salt and pepper

- Place the sausages, onion, carrots, parsnips and garlic in a large, shallow roasting tin. Toss together with the oil and season to taste.

- Place in a preheated oven, 200°C (400°F), Gas Mark 6, for 20 minutes, giving the tin a good shake halfway through cooking. Drizzle over the honey and rosemary, then return to the oven for a further 5–10 minutes until golden and cooked through.

 Creamy Parsnip and Parma Ham Pasta

Cook 1 sliced parsnip in a large saucepan of lightly salted boiling water for 5 minutes, then add 500 g (1 lb) fresh tagliatelle and cook according to the pack instructions until tender. Drain and return the pasta and parsnip to the pan. Stir in 5 tablespoons crème fraîche and 4 slices of Parma ham, cut into strips. Season to taste and serve scattered with thyme leaves.

 Carrot, Parsnip and Sausage

Minestrone Heat 1 tablespoon olive oil in a large, heavy-based saucepan. Add 1 finely chopped onion, 1 chopped carrot and 1 chopped parsnip and cook for 5 minutes until softened. Stir in 1 crushed garlic clove, 1 tablespoon tomato purée, 1.5 litres (2½ pints) chicken stock and a pinch of dried rosemary and simmer for 5 minutes. Add 100 g (3½ oz) shredded kale, a 200 g (7 oz) can cannellini beans, rinsed and drained, and 4 thickly sliced kabanos or other smoked sausages. Season to taste and simmer for a further 5 minutes or until cooked through, then serve with plenty of crusty bread.

Thai Beef Salad with Herbs

Serves 4

5 tablespoons Thai fish sauce
finely grated rind and juice of
½ lime
2 teaspoons caster sugar
1 garlic clove, crushed
1 teaspoon finely grated fresh
root ginger
1 lemon grass stalk, finely chopped
1 red chilli, finely chopped
handful of chopped fresh coriander
handful of chopped mint
1 tablespoon vegetable oil
500 g (1 lb) beef steak
250 g (8 oz) cherry tomatoes
½ cucumber, thinly sliced
handful of salad leaves

- Mix together the fish sauce, lime rind and juice and sugar until the sugar dissolves, then stir in the garlic, ginger, lemon grass, chilli and herbs to make a dressing.

- Rub the oil over the steak and season to taste. Cook in a smoking hot griddle pan for 2–3 minutes on each side, then remove from the pan and cut into slices.

- Place the quartered tomatoes, cucumber and salad leaves on a serving plate, arrange the warm beef on top and drizzle with the dressing. Serve immediately.

2 Thai Beef and Rice with Herbs

Heat 1 tablespoon oil in a nonstick frying pan. Add 2 thinly sliced rump steaks and cook for 1 minute on each side. Set aside. Add more oil to the pan, then cook 1 finely chopped onion for 5 minutes. Stir in 2 teaspoons grated root ginger, 2 crushed garlic cloves and 125 g (4 oz) cherry tomatoes. Cook for 5 minutes, then add 3 tablespoons Thai fish sauce and 1 teaspoon caster sugar. Stir in a handful of chopped basil and fresh coriander, add 300 g (10 oz) ready-cooked rice and heat through. Return the beef to the pan and heat through. Serve with chilli sauce.

3 Thai Beef Lettuce Cups with Herbs

Mix 2 tablespoons Thai fish sauce with ½ chopped red chilli and 1 finely chopped lemon grass stalk. Rub all over 3 beef steaks and set aside to marinate for 20 minutes. Heat a frying pan until smoking hot. Add 1 tablespoon oil, then cook 1 cored, deseeded and sliced red pepper for 1–2 minutes until lightly charred. Remove from the pan and set aside. Add the steaks to the pan, cook for 2–3 minutes on each side, then cut into thick slices. Add the remaining marinade to the pan with another tablespoon fish sauce, a pinch of brown sugar and a little water. Heat until bubbly and syrupy. Break 2 Baby Gem lettuces into leaves and arrange on plates. Place a little chopped cucumber into each leaf, then pile the red pepper and beef on top. Drizzle over the sauce and top with a handful of fresh coriander and mint leaves, to serve.

ONE-MEAT-HEM

30 Pork and Tomato Rice Pot

Serves 4

3 tablespoons olive oil
300 g (10 oz) pork fillet, sliced
1 onion, finely chopped
3 garlic cloves, finely chopped
250 g (8 oz) paella rice
2 teaspoons smoked paprika
200 g (7 oz) can chopped
  tomatoes
650 ml (1 pint 2 fl oz) hot chicken
  stock
125 g (4 oz) baby spinach leaves
salt and pepper
lemon wedges, to serve

• Heat 1 tablespoon of the oil in a large, deep frying pan over a high heat. Add the pork fillet and cook for 3 minutes until golden and nearly cooked through, then remove from the pan and set aside. Reduce the heat, add the onion to the pan with the remaining oil and cook for 3 minutes until softened, then stir in the garlic and cook for 30 seconds.

• Add the rice and cook for 1 minute, then add the paprika and tomatoes, bring to the boil and simmer for 2–3 minutes. Pour in the stock, season to taste and cook for a further 12–15 minutes until there is just a little liquid left around the edges of the pan.

• Lightly fork the spinach through the rice, arrange the pork on top, then cover and continue to cook for 3–4 minutes until cooked through. Serve with lemon wedges for squeezing over.

---

10 Spicy Pork and Tomato Fried Rice

Heat 2 tablespoons vegetable oil in a large wok. Add 300 g (10 oz) pork fillet, cut into strips, and stir-fry for 3 minutes until golden. Stir in 2 sliced garlic cloves and 2 teaspoons finely grated fresh root ginger. Add 2 chopped tomatoes and a pinch of dried chilli flakes, then add 250 g (8 oz) ready-cooked rice and a large handful of chopped basil. Season to taste, heat through and serve immediately.

20 Chorizo, Tomato and Rice Soup

Heat 2 tablespoons olive oil in a large, heavy-based saucepan. Add 125 g (4 oz) thickly sliced chorizo, cook for 2–3 minutes until golden, then add 1 sliced garlic clove. Pour in a 400 g (13 oz) can chopped tomatoes and 1 litre (1¾ pints) hot vegetable stock. Add a pinch of sugar, season to taste and simmer for 10 minutes. Stir in 250 g (8 oz) ready-cooked rice and 100 g (3½ oz) rocket, heat through and serve.

Melting Meatball Sandwiches

Serves 4

1 tablespoon olive oil

300 g (10 oz) small ready-made beef meatballs

350 ml (12 fl oz) ready-made tomato pasta sauce

4 ciabatta rolls

125 g (4 oz) mozzarella cheese, sliced

75 g (3 oz) rocket

salt and pepper

- Heat the oil in a frying pan. Add the meatballs and cook for 5 minutes until browned all over. Pour in the sauce and bring to the boil, then reduce the heat and simmer for 10 minutes. Taste and adjust the seasoning if necessary.

- Lightly toast the ciabattas and split in half. Pile the meatballs and sauce on the bottom halves, top with the mozzarella and cook under a preheated hot grill for 1–2 minutes until starting to melt. Add some rocket, replace the ciabatta tops and serve immediately.

 Italian Steak Sandwiches

Lightly toast 4 large slices of ciabatta bread in a smoking hot griddle pan. Rub 1 tablespoon olive oil over 4 rump steaks, season well and cook in the griddle pan for 2–3 minutes on each side until just cooked through. Arrange the steaks on the bread and top with a handful of sun-blush tomatoes, 75 g (3 oz) rocket and some Parmesan cheese shavings.

 Sloppy Joe Beef Sandwiches

Heat 2 tablespoons oil in a deep frying pan. Add 400 g (13 oz) minced beef and cook for 5 minutes until starting to turn brown. Add 1 chopped onion and cook for a further 5 minutes until softened. Stir in 1 crushed garlic clove, a pinch of chilli powder and 4 tablespoons ready-made barbecue sauce. Pour in a 400 g (13 oz) can chopped tomatoes and 1 cored, deseeded and chopped red pepper, season and simmer for 15 minutes. Split 4 burger buns and spoon some of the mixture inside. Top with grated Cheddar cheese and sliced iceberg lettuce.

ONE-MEAT-HUA

Lamb with Aubergine and Tomato Salad

Serves 4

6 tablespoons olive oil
4 baby aubergines, halved
½ teaspoon ground cumin
½ teaspoon smoked paprika
2 garlic cloves, crushed
finely grated rind and juice of
  ½ lemon
handful of chopped fresh
  coriander
3 tomatoes, chopped
8 lamb chops
salt and pepper

- Rub 2 tablespoons of the oil over the aubergine slices and season well. Heat a griddle pan until smoking hot, then cook the aubergine for about 5 minutes until soft and lightly charred all over.

- Mix the spices, garlic, lemon rind and juice and coriander with 3 tablespoons of the oil, season to taste and toss with the tomatoes and warm aubergine.

- Rub the remaining oil over the lamb and season to taste. Cook in the griddle pan for 3–5 minutes on each side until golden on the outside and still just pink in the middle. Serve with the tomato and aubergine salad.

Grilled Lamb with Aubergine Purée

Drizzle 1 tablespoon olive oil over 8 lamb chops and season to taste. Cook in a smoking hot griddle pan for 3–5 minutes on each side until charred on the outside and still pink in the middle. Meanwhile, remove the skin from 250 g (8 oz) ready-roasted aubergine and place in a food processor with 4 tablespoons natural yogurt and a handful of chopped fresh coriander. Season to taste, blend until smooth and serve with the chops and some crusty bread.

Lamb and Aubergine

Moussaka Heat 3 tablespoons olive oil in a flameproof frying pan. Add 1 sliced aubergine and cook for 5 minutes until softened and golden. Remove from the pan and season to taste. Add more oil to the pan if necessary, then cook 1 finely chopped onion and 300 g (10 oz) minced lamb for 5–10 minutes until softened and golden. Stir in 2 crushed garlic cloves, a pinch of ground cinnamon and 1 tablespoon tomato purée. Add a 400 g (13 oz) can chopped tomatoes, season to taste and simmer for 10 minutes. Arrange the aubergine slices on top of the mince mixture, then spoon over 1 beaten egg mixed with 150 ml (¼ pint) natural yogurt. Sprinkle 25 g (1 oz) grated Parmesan cheese on top and cook under a preheated hot grill for 5 minutes until the topping is set and golden.

30 Beef Stew with Garlic Bread Topping

Serves 4

2 tablespoons olive oil

400 g (13 oz) beef steak, cut into chunks

1 onion, sliced

1 carrot, sliced

1 celery stick, sliced

1 teaspoon tomato purée

2 teaspoons plain flour

handful of chopped thyme

100 ml (3½ fl oz) red wine

200 ml (7 fl oz) hot beef stock

½ ready-made garlic bread baguette, sliced

salt and pepper

- Heat half the oil in a flameproof casserole dish over a high heat. Add the beef and cook for 2–3 minutes until golden, then remove from the pan and set aside. Add the remaining oil and cook the onion, carrot and celery for 5 minutes until softened.

- Stir in the tomato purée, flour and thyme, then pour in the wine and cook for 2–3 minutes until reduced by half. Add the stock and simmer for 15 minutes, then return the meat to the pan.

- Arrange the garlic bread slices on top of the stew, then cook under a preheated hot grill for 3 minutes until the bread is golden and crisp.

 Steaks with Garlic Butter Topping

Mix 50 g (2 oz) softened butter with 1 crushed garlic clove and 1 tablespoon finely grated Parmesan cheese. Heat a griddle pan until smoking hot. Rub 1 tablespoon olive oil over 4 rump steaks and season to taste. Cook in the griddle pan for 2–3 minutes on each side, placing a knob of the flavoured butter on top of each steak for the last minute of cooking. Serve the steaks in crusty baguettes with a handful of shredded lettuce.

 Beef Noodles with Garlic Sauce

Heat 1 tablespoon vegetable oil in a wok. Add 2 thinly sliced rump steaks, stir-fry for 2–3 minutes until browned, then remove from the wok and set aside. Add a little more oil and 1 sliced onion to the wok and cook for 2 minutes until starting to soften, then add 150 g (5 oz) sliced shiitake mushrooms and cook for a further 1 minute. Add 2 sliced garlic cloves and stir-fry until the vegetables are soft. Stir in 75 ml (3 fl oz) oyster sauce and 1 tablespoon soy sauce and simmer for 5 minutes, then add 75 g (3 oz) baby spinach leaves and 250 g (8 oz) ready-cooked rice noodles. Add a splash of water if necessary, return the beef to the pan and cook until heated through.

30 Bacon and Apple Bites

Serves 4

1 tablespoon olive oil, for greasing
1 small onion, sliced
6 bacon rashers, chopped
50 g (2 oz) plain flour
1 egg
150 ml (¼ pint) skimmed milk
2 teaspoons wholegrain mustard
1 apple, sliced
salt and pepper

- Liberally grease a 4-hole Yorkshire pudding tray, with holes 8 cm (3½ inches) across. Divide the onion and bacon between the holes in the tray and cook in a preheated oven, 240°C (475°F), Gas Mark 9, for 5 minutes.

- Meanwhile, place the flour, egg, milk and mustard in a blender, season to taste and blend until smooth.

- Arrange the apple in the holes in the tin, then pour over the batter. Return to the oven for a further 20 minutes or until puffed and golden.

1 Bacon and Apple Salad

Cook 4 streaky bacon rashers and 2 slices of bread under a preheated medium grill for 5–7 minutes, turning once, until golden and crisp. Break the bacon and bread into large pieces. Mix 1 tablespoon apple vinegar, 1 teaspoon mustard and 1 teaspoon runny honey with 3 tablespoons olive oil and season well. Toss the dressing with the bread croûtons, 150 g (5 oz) mixed leaves and 1 sliced Granny Smith apple. Divide between serving plates, then top with the bacon, 25 g (1 oz) shelled walnuts or pecans and 50 g (2 oz) crumbled goats' cheese.

2 Bacon, Apple and Celeriac Soup

Heat 1 tablespoon olive oil in a large, heavy-based saucepan. Add 4 chopped bacon rashers and cook for 2 minutes until golden, then remove from the pan and set aside. Add 1 finely chopped onion to the pan and cook for 2 minutes, then add 1 finely chopped celeriac and 1 small chopped cooking apple. Cook for a further 5 minutes until softened. Pour in 1.5 litres (2½ pints) hot chicken stock and simmer for 7 minutes or until soft. Use a hand-held electric blender to purée the soup until smooth, then season to taste and stir in 4 tablespoons crème fraîche. Ladle the soup into bowls and scatter with the bacon. Mix 4 tablespoons crème fraîche with 2 teaspoons wholegrain mustard, then serve with the soup and some toasted sourdough bread.

30 Lamb Stew with Feta and Pasta

Serves 4

2 tablespoons olive oil

400 g (13 oz) lamb fillet or neck, cut into bite-sized pieces

1 onion, sliced

2 garlic cloves, crushed

1 tablespoon tomato purée

½ teaspoon ground cinnamon

pinch of dried chilli flakes

1 red pepper, cored, deseeded and sliced

750 ml (1¼ pints) hot chicken stock

300 g (10 oz) small soup pasta

salt and pepper

25 g (1 oz) feta cheese, crumbled

handful of chopped parsley, to garnish

- Heat the oil in a large flameproof casserole dish. Add the lamb and cook for 5 minutes until starting to brown, then add the onion and cook for a further 7–8 minutes until soft. Stir in the garlic, tomato purée, spices and red pepper, then pour in the stock.

- Bring to the boil, then reduce the heat and simmer for 1–2 minutes, then add the pasta and cook for 12 minutes, or according to the pack instructions, until the pasta is tender and most of the liquid has boiled away. Season to taste, then serve sprinkled with the feta and parsley.

---

1 Lamb and Feta Pockets

Mix 1 tablespoon olive oil with a pinch of dried oregano and the finely grated rind of 1 lemon then rub over 325 g (11 oz) cubed lamb. Season to taste and cook in a smoking hot griddle pan for 5–7 minutes, turning frequently, until lightly charred. Serve in pitta breads with a handful of shredded cos lettuce, sliced cucumber and halved cherry tomatoes. Drizzle with lemon juice and olive oil, then top with 25 g (1 oz) crumbled feta cheese, 1 chopped red chilli and more dried oregano.

2 Grilled Lamb with Feta and Couscous

Rub 1 tablespoon olive oil all over 8 lamb chops, arrange in a roasting tin and season. Cook under a preheated hot grill for 4 minutes on each side. Scatter 325 g (11 oz) couscous into the tin and pour in 350 ml (12 fl oz) hot chicken stock. Cover tightly with foil and leave for 5 minutes until the couscous is tender. Transfer the chops to serving plates. Fluff up the couscous with a fork and stir in the juice of 1 lemon, a handful of chopped oregano, 1 chopped red chilli, 50 g (2 oz) pitted black olives and 50 g (2 oz) crumbled feta cheese. Serve the couscous with the chops.

Parma Ham and Asparagus Tart

Serves 4

butter, for greasing
300 g (10 oz) ready-rolled
  puff pastry
1 egg, beaten
150 g (5 oz) ricotta cheese
25 g (1 oz) Parmesan cheese,
  grated
150 g (5 oz) fine asparagus spears
4 slices of Parma ham
salt and pepper

- Place the pastry on a baking sheet and use a sharp knife to score a 1 cm (½ inch) border around the edges, making sure you don't cut all the way through the pastry. Prick all over the centre of the pastry using a fork.

- Mix together the ricotta, Parmesan and the remaining beaten egg and season well. Spoon the mixture over the tart, making sure it doesn't spread outside the border. Arrange the asparagus on top. Place in a preheated oven, 220°C (425°F), Gas Mark 7, for 12 minutes.

- Arrange the Parma ham on top of the tart and return to the oven for 5–7 minutes until the pastry is puffed and cooked through.

 Crispy Ham, Asparagus and Rocket Salad Cut 5 Parma ham slices into long strips and wrap around 125 g (4 oz) fine asparagus spears. Drizzle with olive oil and season well with pepper. Cook under a preheated hot grill for 5 minutes, turning once, until golden and crisp. Whisk 1 tablespoon balsamic vinegar with 3 tablespoons olive oil and season. Toss the dressing with 150 g (5 oz) rocket and divide between serving plates. Arrange the ham-wrapped asparagus spears around the rocket, then scatter 50 g (2 oz) crumbled goats' cheese on top.

 Parma Ham and Asparagus Frittata Heat 3 tablespoons olive oil in a flameproof nonstick frying pan. Add 1 sliced potato and cook for 7 minutes until starting to soften, then add 100 g (3½ oz) asparagus tips and cook for a further 5 minutes until the potatoes and asparagus are tender. Whisk 6 eggs with 25 g (1 oz) finely grated Parmesan, season to taste and pour into the pan. Cook over a gentle heat for 15 minutes until the eggs are nearly set. Arrange 4 slices of Parma ham on top and cook under a preheated hot grill for 2–3 minutes until set. Scatter with a handful of chopped basil before serving.

 # Stir-Fried Teriyaki Beef with Noodles and Greens

Serves 4

2 tablespoons vegetable oil

325 g (11 oz) beef fillet, cut into strips

2 garlic cloves, sliced

1 teaspoon finely grated fresh root ginger

125 g (4 oz) spring greens, chopped

300 g (10 oz) ready-cooked udon noodles

4 tablespoons teriyaki sauce

1 tablespoon sesame seeds

- Heat the oil in a large wok. Add the beef strips and cook for 1 minute until browned, then remove from the pan and set aside.

- Add the garlic, ginger and greens to the pan and stir-fry for 2–3 minutes until the greens start to wilt.

- Return the beef to the pan, add the noodles and teriyaki sauce, then cook, adding a little boiling water if necessary, until heated through. Scatter with the sesame seeds and serve immediately.

 Simple Braised Teriyaki Beef

Heat 1 tablespoon oil in a flameproof casserole dish. Add 2 sliced onions and cook over a low heat for 10 minutes until golden. Add 100 ml (3½ fl oz) hot beef stock, 3 tablespoons soy sauce, 2 tablespoons rice wine or dry sherry and 1 tablespoon caster sugar. Simmer for 1–2 minutes, then add 50 g (2 oz) chopped spring greens and cook for a further 2 minutes. Stir in 400 g (13 oz) thinly sliced beef steak and cook for 3 minutes until just cooked. Sprinkle over 1 sliced red chilli before serving with boiled rice, if liked.

 Marinated Teriyaki Beef with Spinach and Radish Salad Mix 2 teaspoons finely grated fresh root ginger with 5 tablespoons teriyaki sauce. Pour over 4 rump steaks and leave to marinate for 20 minutes. Meanwhile, mix 1 tablespoon light miso paste with 3 tablespoons teriyaki sauce, 1 teaspoon finely grated fresh root ginger, 1 teaspoon sesame oil and a little water to make a dressing. Toss with 75 g (3 oz) thinly sliced radishes and 100 g (3½ oz) baby spinach leaves and scatter with 1 tablespoon sesame seeds. Remove the steaks from the

marinade, brush with 1 tablespoon vegetable oil and cook in a preheated hot griddle pan for 2–3 minutes on each side until just cooked through. Leave to rest for a couple of minutes, then cut into thick slices and serve with the salad.

 # Chorizo and Black Bean Soup

Serves 4

2 tablespoons vegetable oil
1 onion, finely chopped
125 g (4 oz) chorizo, finely diced
1 red pepper, cored, deseeded and
    chopped
1 garlic clove, chopped
1 teaspoon ground cumin
1.5 litres (2½ pints) hot chicken
    stock
2 x 400 g (13 oz) cans black
    beans, rinsed and drained
salt and pepper
2 tablespoons lime juice
4 tablespoons soured cream
handful of chopped fresh
    coriander leaves
1 red chilli, chopped

- Heat the oil in a large, heavy-based saucepan. Add the onion, chorizo, red pepper and garlic and cook for 7–10 minutes until soft, then stir in the cumin. Pour in the stock and beans and simmer for 5–8 minutes.

- Season to taste, then use a potato masher to roughly mash some of the beans to thicken the soup. Ladle the soup into bowls and squeeze a little lime juice over each portion. Add a spoonful of soured cream, top with a sprinkling of coriander and chilli and serve immediately.

1 Chorizo and Black Bean Salad

Rinse and drain a 400 g (13 oz) can black beans. Mix with 2 tablespoons extra virgin olive oil and a good squeeze of lime juice. Season to taste and add 2 chopped tomatoes, 2 chopped spring onions and a good handful of chopped fresh coriander. Place on a serving plate and arrange slices of fried chorizo on top. Serve with crusty bread.

3 Chorizo, Black Bean and Sweet Potato Chilli

 Heat 1 tablespoon vegetable oil in a large, heavy-based saucepan. Add 1 finely chopped onion and 75 g (3 oz) chopped chorizo and cook for 5 minutes to soften. Add 1 teaspoon ground cumin, 1 teaspoon smoked paprika and 1 peeled and diced sweet potato, stir well and pour in a 400 g (13 oz) can chopped tomatoes and 200 ml (7 fl oz) water. Simmer for 15 minutes, then add a 400 g (13 oz) can black beans, rinsed and drained. Season to taste and cook for a further 3–5 minutes until heated through, then serve topped with spoonfuls of soured cream and sprinkled with chopped fresh coriander.

30 Lamb and Pomegranate Pilaf

Serves 4

1 tablespoon vegetable oil
400 g (13 oz) lamb fillet, cut into
 chunks
1 onion, finely chopped
1 garlic clove, finely chopped
½ teaspoon ground cinnamon
pinch of allspice
300 g (10 oz) basmati rice
finely grated rind and juice of
 1 orange
850 ml (1 pint 8 fl oz) chicken
 stock
100 g (3½ oz) dried figs, halved
25 g (1 oz) shelled pistachio nuts
handful of chopped mint
handful of chopped parsley
seeds from ½ pomegranate
salt and pepper

- Heat the oil in a large flameproof casserole dish. Add the lamb and cook for 2–3 minutes until browned all over. Add the onion and cook for 5 minutes until softened, then stir in the garlic, cinnamon and allspice. Add the rice and stir until coated.

- Add the orange rind and juice to the pan, followed by the chicken stock and figs, then season to taste. Bring to the boil, then reduce the heat and simmer for 12 minutes until most of the stock has been absorbed.

- Cover tightly and cook over a very low heat for a further 5 minutes until the rice is cooked through. Use a fork to gently stir in the pistachios, herbs and pomegranate seeds, then serve immediately.

---

10 Pomegranate-Glazed Lamb Chops with Salad

Mix 2 tablespoons pomegranate molasses with a good squeeze of lemon juice and a pinch of dried chilli flakes. Rub all over 8 large lamb chops. Cook under a preheated hot grill for 3–4 minutes on each side until charred and just cooked through. Mix 3 tablespoons orange juice with 3 tablespoons olive oil, season and toss with 150 g (5 oz) mixed salad leaves and 4 quartered figs. Scatter the salad with 50 g (2 oz) crumbled feta cheese and serve with the chops.

20 Bulgar Pilaf with Lamb Sausages and Pomegranate

Heat 1 tablespoon olive oil in a deep frying pan. Add 400 g (13 oz) lamb sausages and fry until browned all over, then add 1 crushed garlic clove, 1 chopped red chilli, a pinch of ground cinnamon and 200 g (7 oz) bulgar wheat. Stir in the finely grated rind and juice of 1 orange and 250 ml (8 fl oz) hot chicken stock. Simmer for 10 minutes until the sausages are cooked through and the bulgar is tender. Remove the sausages from the pan and cut into thick slices. Lightly fork a handful of chopped mint and parsley into the pilaf, sprinkle with shelled pistachio nuts and pomegranate seeds and serve with the sausages.

Creamy Ham and Tomato Penne

Serves 4

500 g (1 lb) fresh penne pasta
75 g (3 oz) frozen peas
100 ml (3½ fl oz) crème fraîche
4 slices of ham, torn into
  bite-sized pieces
75 g (3 oz) sun-blush tomatoes
75 g (3 oz) rocket
salt and pepper

- Cook the penne in a large saucepan of lightly salted boiling water according to the pack instructions. Add the frozen peas for the final minute of cooking.

- Drain and return the pasta and peas to the pan, stir in the remaining ingredients and season to taste. Serve immediately.

Creamy Ham and Tomato Soup

Heat 1 tablespoon olive oil in a large, heavy-based saucepan. Add 1 chopped onion and cook for 5 minutes until softened, then add a 400 g (13 oz) can chopped tomatoes, a pinch of sugar and a handful of chopped basil. Simmer for 12 minutes, then use a hand-held electric blender to purée the soup until smooth. Add a little boiling water if it is too thick. Stir in 125 g (4 oz) shredded ham hock and 5 tablespoons crème fraîche, season to taste, heat through and serve with crusty bread.

Pork and Tomato Stew with Creamy Mascarpone

Heat 1 tablespoon olive oil in a flameproof casserole dish over a high heat. Fry 325 g (11 oz) pork tenderloin, cut into thick strips, for 3–5 minutes until golden. You may have to do this in 2 batches. Remove from the pan and set aside. Add 1 chopped onion to the pan and cook for 3 minutes. Stir in 2 crushed garlic cloves and 1 chopped fennel bulb and cook for a further 2–3 minutes more until softened. Pour in 100 ml (3½ fl oz) dry white wine and bring to the boil. Add a 400 g (13 oz) can cherry tomatoes and 300 g (10 oz) small new potatoes and simmer for 12 minutes until the potatoes are tender, then return the pork to the pan, heat through and season to taste. Mix 3 tablespoons mascarpone cheese with a handful of chopped basil, 1 crushed garlic clove and 1 teaspoon finely grated lemon rind. Serve the stew topped with spoonfuls of the mascarpone.

Seared Pork Chops with Chilli Corn

Serves 4

2 tablespoons olive oil

4 pork chops

200 g (7 oz) fresh or canned sweetcorn kernels

2 spring onions, thinly sliced

1 red chilli, chopped

5 tablespoons crème fraîche

finely grated rind of 1 lime

salt and pepper

handful of chopped fresh coriander leaves

- Heat a large frying pan, add half the oil and swirl around the pan. Season the chops to taste and cook in the pan for 5–7 minutes on each side until golden and cooked through. Remove from the pan and keep warm.

- Add the remaining oil to the pan, followed by the sweetcorn. Cook for 2 minutes until starting to brown, then stir in the spring onions and chilli and cook for a further 1 minute. Add the crème fraîche and lime rind and season to taste. Scatter over the coriander and serve with the pork chops.

 Ham and Corn Melts

Spread 100 g (3½ oz) cream cheese over 4 wheat tortillas. Tear up 4 slices of ham and scatter on top with 75 g (3 oz) canned sweetcorn kernels and 25 g (1 oz) grated Cheddar cheese. Place another tortilla on top of each, then cook under a preheated grill for 3 minutes. Carefully turn over and cook for a further 2–3 minutes until the cheese has melted inside.

Bacon and Chilli Cornbread

Heat 2 tablespoons vegetable oil and 50 g (2 oz) butter in an ovenproof frying pan. Add 1 finely chopped onion and 4 chopped bacon rashers and cook for about 3 minutes until softened, then stir in 1 finely chopped red chilli. Meanwhile, place 200 g (7 oz) fine polenta in a food processor with 150 g (5 oz) plain flour, 1 tablespoon sugar, 2 teaspoons baking powder, 1 teaspoon salt, 575 ml (18 fl oz) buttermilk and 1 egg and blend until smooth. Stir in the onions and bacon, then return the mixture to the frying pan and sprinkle 50 g (2 oz) grated Cheddar cheese on top. Bake in a preheated oven, 230°C (450°F), Gas Mark 8, for 25 minutes until just cooked through.

30 Moroccan Lamb Stew

Serves 4

1 tablespoon olive oil

½ onion, chopped

2 garlic cloves, crushed

2 teaspoons finely grated fresh root ginger

2 teaspoons ras el hanout spice mix

400 g (13 oz) can chopped tomatoes

4 eggs

salt and pepper

handful of chopped fresh coriander

For the meatballs

½ onion, grated

400 g (13 oz) minced lamb

1 teaspoon ras el hanout spice mix

1 egg yolk

- First make the meatballs. Squeeze the grated onion to get rid of any excess moisture, then mix with the lamb, ras el hanout and egg yolk and season well. Lightly wet your hands and shape the mixture into 12 meatballs, each about the size of a golf ball.

- Heat the oil in a frying pan. Add the meatballs and cook for 5 minutes until starting to turn golden. Add the chopped onion and cook for 3 minutes until softened, then add the garlic and ginger and cook for a further 1 minute. Stir in the ras el hanout, then pour in the tomatoes. Season to taste and simmer for 12 minutes, topping up with a little water if necessary.

- Make 4 holes in the mixture and crack an egg into each. Loosely cover the pan with foil and simmer for 5 minutes or until the egg whites are just cooked through. Serve scattered with the coriander.

 Moroccan Spiced Lamb Kebabs

Mix 2 teaspoons ras el hanout spice mix with 1 tablespoon olive oil and the finely grated rind of 1 lemon. Rub over 400 g (13 oz) lamb cubes, then thread on to metal skewers. Season to taste and cook under a preheated hot grill for 5–7 minutes, turning often, until golden and cooked through. Serve in toasted pitta breads with some sliced tomatoes and cucumber, a handful of mint leaves and a drizzle of natural yogurt.

 Moroccan Lamb Chops with Griddled Tomatoes and Beans

Mix 2 tablespoons natural yogurt with 1 tablespoon olive oil and 1 teaspoon ras el hanout. Rub over 8 lamb chops and leave to marinate for 10 minutes. Meanwhile, heat a griddle pan until smoking hot. Toss 125 g (4 oz) cherry tomatoes in 2 teaspoons olive oil, season and cook for 2 minutes in the griddle pan until lightly browned. Remove and set aside. Next cook the lamb chops in the preheated griddle pan for 3–5 minutes on each side until lightly charred. Meanwhile, mix 2 x 400 g (13 oz) cans butter beans, rinsed and drained, with 3 tablespoons olive oil, a good squeeze of lemon juice, a handful each of chopped mint and parsley and the griddled tomatoes. Serve the chops with the bean salad and a spoonful of natural yogurt.

1 ⏱ Herby Steak Tortilla Wraps

Serves 4

2 kaffir lime leaves
1 shallot
1 garlic clove
bunch of basil
handful of oregano
1 tablespoon red wine vinegar
5 tablespoons olive oil
1 onion, sliced
4 rump steaks
4 wheat tortillas
5 tablespoons natural yogurt
1 red chilli, chopped
salt and pepper

- Place the lime leaves, shallot, garlic, herbs, vinegar and 4 tablespoons of the oil in a food processor, blend to form a thick sauce and season to taste.

- Toss the onion and steaks with the remaining oil and season well. Heat a griddle pan until smoking hot, add the onion and steaks and cook for 2 minutes. Turn the steaks over and move the onions around the pan and cook for a further 2–3 minutes until cooked to your liking. Remove from the pan and keep warm.

- Warm the tortillas through on the griddle pan. Cut the steaks into thick slices and divide between the tortillas with the onions. Drizzle with the yogurt and herb sauce, then sprinkle with the chilli. Roll up the tortillas neatly and serve immediately.

 Beef Tortilla Wedges

Lay 4 large tortillas on 2 baking sheets. Divide a 400 g (13 oz) can refried beans between them and spread all over. Cut 150 g (5 oz) sliced ready-cooked roast beef into thin strips and scatter on top. Add 2 sliced tomatoes, 50 g (2 oz) grated Cheddar cheese and 75 g (3 oz) sliced mozzarella cheese. Scatter with chopped fresh coriander and top each with another tortilla. Place in a preheated oven, 200°C (400°F), Gas Mark 6, for 10 minutes until golden. Serve cut into wedges.

 Spicy Beef Stew with Tortillas

Heat 1 tablespoon oil in a deep frying pan over a high heat. Add 325 g (11 oz) beef steak, cut into strips, and cook for 1–2 minutes on each side until golden. Remove from the pan and set aside. Add another tablespoon oil to the pan with 1 finely chopped onion and 75 g (3 oz) diced chorizo and cook for 5 minutes until the onion has softened. Stir in 1 crushed garlic clove, 1 teaspoon ground cumin and a pinch of ground cinnamon. Add 1 teaspoon tomato purée, then pour in a 400 g (13 oz) can chopped tomatoes and a pinch of sugar. Simmer for 15 minutes, topping up with water if necessary. Return the beef to the pan, season to taste and heat through. Serve the stew on tortillas, topped with spoonfuls of soured cream, plenty of chopped fresh coriander, some grated Cheddar cheese and a squeeze of lime juice.

30 Sausage and Bean Cassoulet

Serves 4

2 tablespoons olive oil
6 pork sausages
1 onion, chopped
2 garlic cloves, chopped
400 g (13 oz) can chopped
  tomatoes
125 ml (4 fl oz) chicken stock
1 bay leaf
400 g (13 oz) can cannellini beans,
  rinsed and drained
100 g (3½ oz) dried breadcrumbs
handful of chopped parsley
salt and pepper

- Heat 1 tablespoon of the oil in a shallow, flameproof casserole dish. Add the sausages and cook for 5 minutes until starting to turn golden, then add the onion and cook for a further 5 minutes until softened.

- Cut the sausages into thick slices, then return to the pan with the garlic and cook for 1 minute. Add the tomatoes, stock, bay leaf and beans, season to taste and bring to the boil. Reduce the heat and simmer for 5 minutes.

- Mix together the breadcrumbs and thyme and sprinkle over the cassoulet, then drizzle over the remaining oil. Cook in a preheated oven, 200°C (400°F), Gas Mark 6, for 10–12 minutes until the topping is golden and crisp.

 10 Warm Chorizo and Bean Salad

Heat 2 tablespoons olive oil in a deep frying pan. Add 125 g (4 oz) sliced thick chorizo sausage and cook for 3 minutes until starting to turn golden then add 2 sliced garlic cloves and cook for a further 1 minute. Stir in 125 g (4 oz) halved cherry tomatoes and cook for 1–2 minutes until starting to soften. Add a 400 g (13 oz) can cannellini beans, rinsed and drained, and heat through. Season to taste, scatter with chopped parsley and serve.

 20 Creamy White Bean and Sausage

Bake Mix together 4 sliced cooked smoked sausages, 2 x 400 g (13 oz) cans cannellini beans, rinsed and drained, 125 ml (4 fl oz) crème fraîche, 75 ml (3 fl oz) hot vegetable stock and a handful of chopped thyme. Tip into an ovenproof dish and top with 75 g (3 oz) dried breadcrumbs and 25 g (1 oz) grated Gruyère cheese. Place in a preheated oven, 220°C (425°F), Gas Mark 7, for 15 minutes until golden and bubbling.

ONE-MEAT-CUW

Rosemary-Crusted Roast Lamb

Serves 4

750 g (1½ lb) small new potatoes, halved

300 g (10 oz) small chantenay carrots

3 tablespoons olive oil

3 tablespoons Dijon mustard

2 garlic cloves, crushed

2 racks of lamb, 7–8 bones each

1 tablespoon chopped rosemary

50 g (2 oz) dried breadcrumbs

2 teaspoons balsamic vinegar

2 tablespoons redcurrant jelly

75 ml (3 fl oz) chicken or lamb stock

salt and pepper

- Toss the potatoes and carrots with 2 tablespoons of the oil and season well. Place in a large, shallow roasting tin and cook in a preheated oven, 220°C (425°F), Gas Mark 7, for 5 minutes.

- Meanwhile, mix the remaining oil with the mustard and garlic and season to taste. Spread over the skin of the lamb, then scatter the rosemary and breadcrumbs on top and press lightly into place.

- Arrange the lamb racks in the roasting tin and cook for 20 minutes until the vegetables are tender and the lamb is cooked to your liking, then remove the lamb and vegetables from the tin and keep warm.

- Place the roasting tin over a gentle heat on the hob and add the balsamic vinegar, redcurrant jelly and stock. Allow to bubble for 2 minutes, then serve with the meat and vegetables.

 Grilled Lamb and Rosemary Skewers

Mix together the finely grated rind of 1 lemon, 1 teaspoon chopped rosemary and 1 tablespoon olive oil. Rub over 400 g (13 oz) lamb cubes, then thread on to metal skewers. Season to taste and cook under a preheated hot grill for 5–7 minutes, turning often, until golden and cooked through. Serve in toasted baguettes with redcurrant jelly and a large handful of lambs' lettuce.

 Greek Roast Lamb with Rosemary

Place 4 thick lamb steaks in a roasting tin with 200 g (7 oz) halved tomatoes and 2 cored, deseeded and sliced red peppers. Drizzle over 1 tablespoon olive oil, sprinkle with 2 teaspoons chopped oregano and 1 teaspoon chopped rosemary and season well. Place in a preheated oven, 200°C (400°F), Gas Mark 6, for 15 minutes until the lamb is cooked through. Stir in a 400 g (13 oz) can butter beans, rinsed and drained. Serve scattered with chopped parsley and 50 g (2 oz) crumbled feta cheese.

20 🕐 Italian Beefburgers with Polenta Chips

Serves 4

1 shallot, finely chopped
1 egg yolk
450 g (14½ oz) minced beef
4 tablespoons olive oil
500 g (1 lb) ready-made polenta,
  cut into chips
125 g (4 oz) mozzarella cheese,
  sliced
4 tomatoes, chopped
2 teaspoons balsamic vinegar
handful of chopped basil
4 ciabatta rolls, lightly toasted
handful of rocket
salt and pepper

- Mix together three-quarters of the shallot, the egg yolk and beef and season well. Wet your hands and shape the mixture into 4 burgers. Brush all over with a little oil, place on a baking sheet and cook under a preheated hot grill for 5 minutes until golden.

- Turn the burgers over, arrange the polenta chips on the baking sheet and drizzle with a little more oil. Cook for a further 3 minutes, then turn over the polenta chips and place the mozzarella on top of the burgers. Return to the grill for 1–2 minutes until the cheese has melted and the polenta is golden.

- Meanwhile, mix together the tomatoes, the remaining shallot and oil, the balsamic vinegar and basil and season to taste. Place the burgers in the buns with a handful of rocket and serve with the tomato salad and polenta chips.

 Italian Griddled Beef Sandwiches

Rub 1 tablespoon olive oil all over 4 rump steaks and season well. Cook in a smoking hot griddle pan for 2–3 minutes on each side. Mix 2 tablespoons pesto with 4 tablespoons mayonnaise and spread on 4 slices of lightly toasted sourdough bread. Cut the steaks into thin strips and arrange on the bread, then chop 2 tomatoes and scatter on top with a sprinkling of basil leaves. Serve immediately.

 Italian Stewed Beef

Heat 2 tablespoons olive oil in a large, heavy-based saucepan over a high heat. Add 400 g (13 oz) beef, cut into strips, and cook for 2–3 minutes until golden, then remove from the pan and set aside. Reduce the heat, add 1 chopped onion to the pan and cook for 5 minutes until softened, then stir in 1 cored, deseeded and sliced yellow pepper, 2 crushed garlic cloves, 2 teaspoons tomato purée and a pinch each of dried chilli flakes and dried oregano. Pour in 100 ml (3½ fl oz) dry white wine and simmer for 3 minutes, then add a 400 g (13 oz) can chopped tomatoes. Bring to the boil, then reduce the heat and simmer for 15 minutes. Return the beef to the pan and cook for a further 3 minutes until heated through, then serve with ciabatta bread.

30 Roast Pork with Fennel and Lemon

Serves 4

2 x 375 g (12 oz) pork tenderloins
2 tablespoons olive oil
2 lemons
750 g (1½ lb) small new potatoes, halved
1 fennel bulb, sliced
3–4 sage leaves
salt and pepper

- Rub the pork with a little of the oil and place in a large, shallow roasting tin. Finely grate the rind of 1 lemon and sprinkle over the pork with salt and lots of pepper.

- Scatter the potatoes around the pork and drizzle over the remaining oil. Place in a preheated oven, 220°C (425°F), Gas Mark 7 for 10 minutes.

- Cut the other lemon into wedges and add to the roasting tin with the fennel and sage leaves. Return to the oven for 15 minutes until the meat and potatoes are cooked through.

 Pork Chops with Fennel and Lemon Coleslaw Rub a pinch of chilli powder and 1 tablespoon olive oil over 4 pork chops and season well. Heat a griddle pan until smoking hot, then cook the pork for 4 minutes on each side until golden and cooked through. Meanwhile, finely slice 2 fennel bulbs and mix with 5 tablespoons mayonnaise, 1 tablespoon lemon juice and a handful of chopped parsley. Serve the coleslaw with the chops.

 Fennel and Lemon Porkballs with Cannellini Beans Mix 400 g (13 oz) minced pork with the finely grated rind of 1 lemon, 1 teaspoon crushed fennel seeds, ½ finely chopped red chilli, 50 g (2 oz) fresh white breadcrumbs and 1 egg yolk. Season to taste and use wet hands to shape into 12 balls. Heat 1 tablespoon olive oil in a flameproof casserole dish. Fry the balls for 5 minutes until golden, then add 250 ml (8 fl oz) hot chicken stock and simmer for 5 minutes. Add 125 g (4 oz) halved cherry tomatoes and a 400 g (13 oz) can cannellini beans, rinsed and drained. Cook for a further 5 minutes until heated through, then serve scattered with chopped basil.

ONE-MEAT-RET

1 Herby Ham and Lentil Salad

Serves 4

1 shallot, finely chopped

2 tablespoons extra virgin olive oil

finely grated rind and juice of
½ lemon

handful of chopped parsley

250 g (8 oz) can lentils, rinsed
and drained

1 teaspoon capers, rinsed and
drained

150 g (5 oz) pulled ham hock

125 g (4 oz) cherry tomatoes,
halved

100 g (3½ oz) rocket

- Mix together the shallot, oil, lemon rind and juice and parsley and then stir the mixture into the lentils.

- Add the capers, ham, tomatoes and rocket. Season to taste and arrange on a platter to serve.

---

2 Spicy Ham and Lentil Wraps

Heat 1 tablespoon vegetable oil in a large, heavy-based saucepan. Add 2 crushed garlic cloves, 1 teaspoon ground cumin, 1 teaspoon ground paprika and ½ teaspoon ground coriander and cook for 30 seconds, then add a 200 g (7 oz) can chopped tomatoes and 100 ml (3½ fl oz) water, season to taste and simmer for 10 minutes. Add a 400 g (13 oz) can lentils, rinsed and drained, and 75 g (3 oz) pulled ham hock and cook for 5 minutes, then stir in a large handful of chopped fresh coriander. Heat 4 wheat tortillas briefly in an oven or microwave, then spoon the sauce over them and fold up to make parcels.

3 Gammon and Lentil Soup with Rocket Salsa Verde

Heat 2 tablespoons olive oil in a large, heavy-based saucepan. Add 1 chopped onion, 1 chopped carrot and 1 chopped celery stick and cook for 5 minutes until softened, then add 1.5 litres (2½ pints) hot chicken stock and 250 g (8 oz) smoked gammon steaks, cut into bite-sized pieces. Bring to the boil, then reduce the heat and simmer for 10 minutes. Add a 400 g (13 oz) can lentils, rinsed and drained, season to taste and cook for a further 2 minutes, until soft. Meanwhile, place 100 g (3½ oz) rocket in a food processor with 1 crushed garlic clove, 1 teaspoon capers, rinsed and drained, 1 tablespoon lemon juice and 4 tablespoons extra virgin olive oil and blend until smooth. Serve the soup drizzled with the salsa verde.

30 Spicy Beef and Squash Stew with Sweetcorn

Serves 4

2 tablespoons vegetable oil

2 large beef steaks, cut into chunks

1 onion, finely chopped

1 small butternut squash, peeled and cut into chunks

1 red chilli, deseeded and chopped

1 teaspoon ground cumin

1 tablespoon tomato purée

400 g (13 oz) can cherry tomatoes

150 g (5 oz) canned sweetcorn kernels

handful of chopped fresh coriander, to garnish

- Heat half the oil in a large, heavy-based saucepan. Add the steak and cook over a high heat for about 3 minutes until browned, then remove from the pan and set aside.

- Add the remaining oil to the pan with the onion and squash and cook for 5 minutes until softened. Stir in the chilli and cumin and cook for 30 seconds, then add the tomato purée and tomatoes and simmer for 15 minutes.

- Return the beef to the pan with the sweetcorn and heat through. Serve scattered with the coriander.

 Seared Beef and Tomatoes with Polenta Heat 2 tablespoons oil in a nonstick frying pan. Add 500 g (1 lb) thickly sliced ready-cooked polenta and cook for 1 minute on each side until golden. Season to taste, remove from the pan and keep warm. Add 4 small beef steaks to the pan and cook for 2 minutes. Turn the steaks over and add 125 g (4 oz) halved cherry tomatoes to the pan. Cook for 2–3 minutes until the steaks are cooked to your liking. Season to taste, sprinkle with chopped basil and spoon over the polenta slices to serve.

 Beef, Tomato and Beans with Nacho Topping Heat 1 tablespoon oil in a large, flameproof frying pan. Add 1 finely chopped onion and cook for 2 minutes, then stir in 300 g (10 oz) minced beef. Cook for 5 minutes until golden, then add 1 teaspoon each of ground coriander and cumin. Stir in a 200 g (7 oz) can chopped tomatoes and simmer for 10 minutes, topping up with a little water if necessary. Add 200 g (7 oz) canned kidney beans, rinsed and drained, and heat through. Arrange 75 g (3 oz) tortilla chips on top of the stew and scatter with 50 g (2 oz) grated Cheddar cheese. Cook under a preheated hot grill for 1–2 minutes until the cheese melts. Serve with soured cream, guacamole and salsa.

30 Pork and Paprika Goulash

Serves 4

2 tablespoons vegetable oil
400 g (13 oz) pork loin, cubed
1 onion, sliced
2 teaspoons smoked paprika
400 g (13 oz) can chopped
  tomatoes
500 g (1 lb) potatoes, diced
salt and pepper
4 tablespoons soured cream
handful of chopped parsley,
  to garnish

- Heat half the oil in a deep frying pan. Add the pork, season to taste and cook for 5 minutes until browned all over. Remove from the pan and set aside. Add the remaining oil to the pan with the onion and cook for 5 minutes until softened.

- Stir in the paprika, then add the tomatoes and potatoes. Season to taste, bring to the boil, then reduce the heat and simmer for 10 minutes.

- Return the pork to the pan and cook for a further 5 minutes until the pork and potatoes are cooked through. Divide between serving bowls, top with the soured cream and serve sprinkled with parsley.

---

10 Chorizo and Roasted Pepper Sandwiches with Paprika Heat a griddle pan until smoking hot, then cook 2 red peppers, cored, deseeded and cut into thick wedges, for 3–4 minutes until charred. Remove the peppers from the pan and set aside. Add a 200 g (7 oz) cooked chorizo sausage, halved lengthways, to the pan and cook for 1–2 minutes until browned. Lightly toast 4 ciabatta rolls and rub the cut surfaces with a peeled garlic clove. Cut the peppers and chorizo into slices and divide between the rolls. Top with a handful of rocket, a little soured cream and a sprinkling of smoked paprika.

20 Crispy Paprika Pork Chops with Roasted Peppers Mix 75 g (3 oz) dried breadcrumbs with the finely grated rind of ½ lemon and 2 teaspoons smoked paprika. Dip 4 pork chops into olive oil, then press into the breadcrumb mixture and season to taste. Arrange the chops on a baking sheet with 2 sliced red peppers. Place in a preheated oven, 220°C (425°F), Gas Mark 7, for 15 minutes until the pork is cooked through, then serve with a green salad.

Sweet Potato and Chorizo Hash

Serves 4

3 tablespoons olive oil

125 g (4 oz) chorizo, thickly sliced

1 onion, sliced

3 sweet potatoes, peeled
   and diced

4 tablespoons fresh green pesto

1 tablespoon lemon juice

2 teaspoons capers, rinsed
   and drained

125 g (4 oz) rocket

salt and pepper

- Heat 1 tablespoon of the oil in a large nonstick frying pan. Add the chorizo and cook for 2 minutes until golden, then remove from the pan and set aside.

- Add the onion to the pan and cook for 3 minutes until starting to soften, then add the sweet potatoes. Cook gently for a further 10 minutes until the sweet potatoes are tender, then season to taste. Return the chorizo to the pan and heat through.

- Mix the pesto with the lemon juice and capers. Serve the rocket with the sweet potato hash and drizzle over the pesto.

 ### Sweet Potato Pasta with Chorizo

Cook 400 g (13 oz) quick-cook penne pasta in a large saucepan of lightly salted boiling water according to the pack instructions, adding 2 peeled and diced sweet potatoes for the last 6 minutes of cooking. Drain and return the pasta and sweet potatoes to the pan. Add 75 g (3 oz) very thin chorizo slices, cut into quarters, the finely grated rind and juice of ½ lemon, 3 tablespoons olive oil and 75 g (3 oz) rocket. Season to taste and serve immediately.

 ### Sweet Potato and Chorizo Soup

Heat 1 tablespoon olive oil in a large, heavy-based saucepan. Add 125 g (4 oz) diced chorizo and cook for 2 minutes until golden, then remove from the pan and set aside. Add 1 finely chopped onion to the pan and cook for 5 minutes until softened, then add 3 chopped sweet potatoes, cover and cook gently for 10 minutes until tender. Add 1 crushed garlic clove and a pinch of dried chilli flakes, then pour in 1.5 litres (2½ pints) vegetable stock.

Simmer for 10 minutes, then use a hand-held electric blender to purée the soup until smooth. Stir in 5 tablespoons crème fraîche, then ladle the soup into warmed serving bowls and scatter with the chorizo to serve.

ONE-MEAT-FOE

QuickCook
Vegetarian

Recipes listed by cooking time

30

2

10

30 Crispy Spinach and Feta Pie

Serves 4

250 g (8 oz) frozen leaf spinach
2 spring onions, chopped
1 garlic clove, crushed
200 g (7 oz) feta cheese,
  crumbled
2 eggs, beaten
pinch of grated nutmeg
25 g (1 oz) butter, melted
3 tablespoons olive oil
5 large filo pastry sheets
salt and pepper

- Place the spinach in a sieve then pour over boiling water from the kettle to defrost. Squeeze to remove excess water, then mix with the spring onions, garlic, feta and eggs. Add the nutmeg and season to taste.

- Stir together the butter and oil and brush over the sides and base of a 20 cm (8 inch) springform cake tin. Unwrap the filo pastry and cover with a piece of damp kitchen paper until ready to use it.

- Working quickly, brush 1 sheet with the butter mixture and arrange in the tin, letting the excess pastry hang over the sides. Brush another sheet with the butter mixture, turn the tin a little and arrange it in the same way. Repeat until the bottom and sides of the tin are completely covered.

- Spoon the filling into the tin, then fold the pastry edges in to cover the filling, scrunching them up a bit as you go. Brush the top of the pie with a little more butter mixture and cook in a preheated oven, 200°C (400°F), Gas Mark 6, for 20–25 minutes until golden and crisp.

 Spinach, Feta and Chickpea Salad
Whisk together 1 tablespoon lemon juice, 3 tablespoons olive oil and a pinch of ground cumin. Toss with a 400 g (13 oz) can chickpeas, rinsed and drained, and ½ thinly sliced red onion and season well. Stir in 125 g (4 oz) baby spinach leaves and 1 chopped ready-roasted red pepper and arrange on a serving plate. Crumble over 75 g (3 oz) feta cheese and serve.

 Spinach Pancakes with Tomato and Feta Salsa Place 200 g (7 oz) self-raising flour and 1 teaspoon baking powder in a mixing bowl. Stir in 1 egg, 300 ml (½ pint) milk and a good pinch of salt, then beat until smooth. Add 75 g (3 oz) finely chopped spinach. Heat a large, nonstick frying pan, add 1 tablespoon butter and swirl around the pan. Drop heaped tablespoons of the batter into the pan and cook for 2–3 minutes on each side until puffed and set. Keep warm while you cook the remainder. Meanwhile, mix together 3 chopped tomatoes, 125 g (4 oz) crumbled feta cheese, a handful of chopped oregano, 2 tablespoons olive oil and 1 teaspoon red wine vinegar. Season to taste and spoon over the pancakes to serve.

ONE-VEGE-DAW

 # Sweet Potato and Coconut Curry

Serves 4

1 tablespoon vegetable oil

1 onion, chopped

2 garlic cloves, crushed

1 tablespoon finely grated fresh
  root ginger

2 tablespoons Thai red curry paste

400 ml (14 fl oz) coconut milk

200 ml (7 fl oz) hot vegetable
  stock

1 teaspoon caster sugar

1 tablespoon Thai fish sauce

2 lemon grass stalks

3 sweet potatoes, peeled and
  diced

2 large tomatoes, quartered

salt and pepper

2 tablespoons lime juice

handful of chopped fresh coriander

25 g (1 oz) bean sprouts

- Heat the oil in a large, heavy-based saucepan. Add the onion and cook for 3–5 minutes until softened. Stir in the garlic and ginger, followed by the curry paste, and cook for 1 minute. Add the coconut milk, stock, sugar, fish sauce and lemon grass and bring to the boil.

- Add the sweet potatoes to the pan and simmer for 10 minutes until tender, then add the tomatoes and cook for a further 2 minutes. Divide the curry between warmed bowls, pour over the lime juice and top with the coriander and bean sprouts to serve.

 ### Sweet Potato and Coconut Soup

Heat 1 tablespoon vegetable oil in a large saucepan. Add 1 crushed garlic clove, 2 teaspoons grated root ginger and 2 teaspoons Thai red curry paste. Cook for 30 seconds, then add 2 finely chopped sweet potatoes. Pour in 200 ml (7 fl oz) coconut milk and 1 litre (1¾ pints) hot vegetable stock, bring to the boil and cook for 7 minutes until tender. Use a hand-held electric blender to purée the soup until smooth. Sprinkle with chopped coriander.

 ### Sweet Potato, Coconut and Lemon Grass Risotto

Heat 1 tablespoon vegetable oil in a deep frying pan. Add 1 peeled and finely chopped sweet potato and cook for 5 minutes until golden. Remove from the pan and set aside. Add 1 finely chopped onion to the pan, with a little more oil if necessary, and cook for 5 minutes until softened. Stir in 2 crushed garlic cloves and 1 teaspoon finely grated fresh root ginger, cook for 30 seconds, then add 300 g (10 oz) risotto rice. Stir well, then add 300 ml (½ pint) hot vegetable stock, 2 lemon grass stalks and 2 kaffir lime leaves. Simmer, stirring continuously, until the liquid has been absorbed, then add 400 ml (14 fl oz) coconut milk. When the rice is beginning to dry out again, return the sweet potato to the pan and add another 300 ml (½ pint) stock. Continue to cook, adding more stock if necessary, until the rice is tender. Season to taste and serve scattered with chopped fresh coriander.

ONE-VEGE-MYL

30 Tomato and Basil Tart

Serves 4

butter for greasing
375 g (12 oz) ready-made
   puff pastry
plain flour, for dusting
1 egg, beaten
200 g (7 oz) mascarpone cheese
50 g (2 oz) Parmesan cheese,
   grated
handful of chopped basil, plus
   extra to garnish
150 g (5 oz) cherry tomatoes,
   halved
1 tablespoon olive oil
salt and pepper

- Lightly grease a baking sheet. Roll out the pastry to a 30 cm (12 inch) disc. Place on the baking sheet and roll the edges up to create a 1 cm (½ inch) border.

- Press the border down with your thumb to make a crumpled edge, then prick over the middle of the pastry disc a few times with a fork. Place in the freezer for a few minutes.

- Brush the border of the pastry with a little of the beaten egg. Mix together the mascarpone, remaining egg, Parmesan and basil, season to taste and spread over the centre of the tart. Top with the tomatoes and drizzle over the oil.

- Place in a preheated oven, 220°C (425°F), Gas Mark 7, for 20–25 minutes until golden and crisp.

 10 Tomato and Basil Omelettes

Beat 1 tablespoon fresh green pesto with 4 eggs. Heat 1 teaspoon butter in a small frying pan and add one-quarter of the egg mixture. Stir for 10 seconds, then leave to set. Sprinkle over a little grated Parmesan cheese and 3 halved cherry tomatoes. Fold over and keep warm, then repeat to make 4 omelettes in all. Serve with new potatoes and mixed salad leaves, if liked.

 20 Creamy Tomato and Basil Soup

Heat 2 tablespoons olive oil in a large, heavy-based saucepan. Add 1 finely chopped onion and cook for 5 minutes until softened. Add a 400 g (13 oz) can chopped tomatoes and 1 litre (1¾ pints) hot vegetable stock and bring to the boil, then reduce the heat and simmer for 10 minutes. Stir in a handful of chopped basil, then use a hand-held electric blender to purée the soup until smooth. Add 75 ml (3 fl oz) double cream, season, heat through and serve with ciabatta rolls, if liked.

ONE-VEGE-BEF

Zingy Wild Mushroom Rice

Serves 4

25 g (1 oz) butter
1 tablespoon olive oil
200 g (7 oz) wild mushrooms,
  roughly chopped
1 onion, finely chopped
2 garlic cloves, crushed
250 g (8 oz) mixed wild and
  basmati rice
750 ml (1¼ pints) vegetable stock
finely grated rind and juice of
  1 lemon
2 spring onions, chopped
large handful of chopped parsley
½ red chilli, chopped
salt and pepper

- Heat the butter and oil in a large, heavy-based saucepan. Add the mushrooms and cook for 3 minutes until golden, then remove from the pan and set aside. Add the onion to the pan and cook for 5 minutes until softened, then stir in the garlic. Add the rice and stir until coated in the oil, then pour in the stock.

- Bring to the boil, then reduce the heat and simmer for about 15 minutes until most of the liquid has been absorbed. Return the mushrooms to the pan, cover and cook very gently for 5–7 minutes until the rice is tender. Season to taste and stir in the remaining ingredients before serving.

Thai Mushroom and Rice Noodle Soup

Heat 1 tablespoon vegetable oil in a large saucepan. Add 1 tablespoon Thai red curry paste and cook for 30 seconds. Add 1.5 litres (2½ pints) hot vegetable stock, 1 lemon grass stalk and 150 g (5 oz) shiitake mushrooms, halved if large. Simmer for 3 minutes, then add 250 g (8 oz) ready-cooked rice noodles. Heat through, divide between serving bowls and serve topped with a handful of bean sprouts and chopped fresh coriander.

Mushroom and Rice Cakes

Heat 1 tablespoon butter and 1 tablespoon olive oil in a nonstick frying pan. Add 1 crushed garlic clove and 150 g (5 oz) finely chopped mushrooms and cook for 5 minutes. Remove from the pan and cool. Mix the mushrooms with 1 egg yolk, 300 g (10 oz) ready-cooked rice, 25 g (1 oz) grated Parmesan cheese, the finely grated rind of ½ lemon, a pinch of dried chilli flakes and a handful of chopped parsley. Season to taste and shape into small cakes with your hands, then lightly coat with a little flour. Heat a little more oil in the frying pan, then cook the cakes for 3 minutes on each side until golden and cooked through. Serve with a tomato salad.

 # Chickpea and Red Pepper Soup

Serves 4

2 tablespoons olive oil
1 onion, finely chopped
1 red pepper, cored, deseeded and
  chopped
2 garlic cloves, crushed
2 teaspoons tomato purée
1 teaspoon ground cumin
½ teaspoon ground coriander
pinch of cayenne pepper
pinch of saffron threads
1.5 litres (2½ pints) hot vegetable
  stock
400 g (13 oz) can chickpeas,
  rinsed and drained
125 g (4 oz) couscous
finely grated rind and juice of
  1 lemon
salt and pepper
handful of chopped mint
handful of chopped fresh coriander

- Heat the oil in a large, heavy-based saucepan. Add the onion and cook for 5 minutes, then add the red pepper, garlic, tomato purée and spices and cook for a further 1 minute.

- Pour in the stock and bring to the boil, then reduce the heat and simmer for 5 minutes. Add the chickpeas and simmer for a further 5 minutes, then season to taste.

- Add the couscous and a squeeze of lemon juice and cook for 1 minute until the couscous is tender. Divide between serving bowls and sprinkle with the herbs and grated lemon rind before serving.

 Chickpea and Red Pepper Couscous

Heat 1 tablespoon olive oil in a large, heavy-based saucepan. Add 2 sliced garlic cloves and cook for 1 minute, then add 1 chopped ready-roasted pepper, 200 g (7 oz) canned chickpeas, rinsed and drained, and 200 g (7 oz) couscous. Remove from the heat. Pour in 250 ml (8 fl oz) hot vegetable stock, cover and leave for 5 minutes until tender. Stir in a good squeeze of lemon juice and 75 g (3 oz) rocket.

 Chickpea and Red Pepper Burgers

Place 2 x 400 g (13 oz) cans chickpeas, rinsed and well drained, in a food processor with 1 crushed garlic clove, the finely grated rind of ½ lemon, a handful of mint leaves, 50 g (2 oz) dried breadcrumbs and 1 egg yolk and blend to form a rough paste. Finely chop 1 ready-roasted red pepper and stir in, then shape the mixture into 4 large patties. Chill in the refrigerator for 15 minutes. Heat 2 tablespoons olive oil in a nonstick frying pan. Add the burgers and cook for 3 minutes on each side until golden. Serve in lightly toasted buns with sliced tomatoes and a handful of coriander leaves. Add a drizzle of tahini, if liked.

ONE-VEGE-DED

30 Squash with Stilton Fondue

Serves 4

4 Little Gem or other small
  squash
1 tablespoon olive oil
200 g (7 oz) crème fraîche
1 tablespoon cornflour
200 g (7 oz) Stilton or other blue
  cheese, rind removed
handful of thyme leaves
salt and pepper

- Cut the squash in half and trim a thin slice off the rounded back of each half so they will stand securely, cut sides up. Scoop out and discard the seeds and fibres, then score the cut surface of the squash in a criss-cross pattern. Drizzle over the oil and season to taste. Arrange on a baking sheet and cook in a preheated oven, 230°C (450°F), Gas Mark 8, for 15 minutes until tender.

- Meanwhile, mix together the crème fraîche and cornflour, then mash in the Stilton with a fork and add plenty of black pepper. Divide the mixture between the cavities of the squash halves, scatter over the thyme leaves and return to the oven for a further 10 minutes until the filling is golden and bubbling.

 ### 1 Squash, Stilton and Spinach Pasta

Cook 1 small butternut squash, peeled and diced, and 400 g (13 oz) spaghetti in a large saucepan of lightly salted boiling water for 9 minutes or according to the pack instructions. Add 125 g (4 oz) baby spinach leaves and drain straight away, then return the spaghetti and vegetables to the pan. Stir in 5 tablespoons crème fraîche and 50 g (2 oz) crumbled Stilton, season to taste and serve immediately.

 ### 2 Squash and Stilton Frittata

Heat 4 tablespoons olive oil in a large nonstick frying pan. Add 1 sliced red onion and 1 small butternut squash, peeled and diced, and cook for 5 minutes until softened. Beat 5 eggs with 2 finely chopped sage leaves and season well. Reduce the heat to low, then pour the eggs into the pan. Crumble 50 g (2 oz) Stilton over the top, then cook very gently for 10–15 minutes until the eggs are just set.

ONE-VEGE-TAU

 2 Sweetcorn, Coconut and Tomato Curry

Serves 4

1 tablespoon vegetable oil

1 onion, finely chopped

2 garlic cloves, finely chopped

1 tablespoon grated fresh root ginger

1 teaspoon mustard seeds

1 teaspoon cumin seeds

1 teaspoon ground coriander

½ teaspoon ground turmeric

400 g (13 oz) can chopped tomatoes

200 ml (7 fl oz) coconut milk

4 sweetcorn cobs, cut into thick slices

salt and pepper

handful of chopped fresh coriander, to garnish

- Heat the oil in a large, flameproof casserole dish. Add the onion and cook for 5 minutes until softened. Stir in the garlic, ginger and whole spices and cook for 1 minute until the spices start to sizzle.

- Add the ground spices, stir well, then add the tomatoes and coconut milk. Bring to the boil, then reduce the heat and simmer for 10 minutes.

- Season to taste, add the sweetcorn and cook for 2–3 minutes until just tender. Serve scattered with the coriander.

 Sweetcorn and Coconut Soup

Place 1 small crushed garlic clove in a heavy-based saucepan with 2 chopped spring onions, 150 g (5 oz) canned sweetcorn kernels, 1 chopped red chilli, 200 ml (7 fl oz) coconut milk and 1 litre (1¾ pints) hot vegetable stock. Bring to the boil, reduce the heat and simmer for 8 minutes. Use a hand-held electric blender to purée the soup until smooth. Drizzle over 2 tablespoons lime juice and scatter with fresh coriander leaves to serve.

 Creamy Sweetcorn and Coconut Bake

Pour 400 ml (14 fl oz) coconut milk into an ovenproof frying pan, add 50 g (2 oz) polenta, 125 g (4 oz) canned sweetcorn kernels and 25 g (1 oz) butter and season to taste. Simmer gently for 5 minutes until starting to thicken, then set aside to cool for 5 minutes. Meanwhile, whisk 4 egg whites until stiff peaks form. Beat the 4 egg yolks into the sweetcorn mixture, one at a time, then gently fold in the egg whites until well combined. Place in a preheated oven, 220 °C (425 °F), Gas Mark 7, for 15–20 minutes until risen and golden. Serve immediately.

ONE-VEGE-GOB

30 Pea and Asparagus Risotto

Serves 4

1 tablespoon olive oil
1 onion, finely chopped
1 garlic clove, crushed
300 g (10 oz) risotto rice
125 ml (4 fl oz) dry white wine
1 litre (1¾ pints) hot vegetable
  stock
125 g (4 oz) fine asparagus spears,
  halved
75 g (3 oz) frozen peas
25 g (1 oz) butter
salt and pepper
50 g (2 oz) rocket
Parmesan cheese shavings

- Heat the oil in a large, heavy-based saucepan. Add the onion and cook for 5 minutes until softened. Add the garlic and rice and cook for 30 seconds until coated in the oil. Pour in the wine and bubble until boiled away.

- Gradually add the stock, a ladleful at a time, stirring continuously and allowing each ladleful to be absorbed before adding the next. After 10 minutes, add the asparagus, then cook for a further 5 minutes until the rice is tender.

- Stir in the peas and butter, cover and leave to stand for 1–2 minutes. Season the risotto taste, then spoon into warmed bowls and top each portion with a handful of rocket and some Parmesan shavings.

 Pea and Mushroom Fried Rice

Heat 1 tablespoon vegetable oil in a deep frying pan. Add 150 g (5 oz) halved shiitake mushrooms and cook for 2 minutes until softened. Add 2 sliced spring onions, 125 g (4 oz) mangetout, 1 crushed garlic clove and 1 teaspoon grated fresh root ginger. Cook for 1 minute, then add 300 g (10 oz) ready-cooked rice and 75 g (3 oz) frozen peas. Cook for 2 minutes, then push the mixture to the sides of the pan. Crack an egg into the centre and stir to scramble.

When set, stir the egg into the rice with 2–3 tablespoons soy sauce and serve immediately.

 Pea, Asparagus and Rice Soup

Heat 2 tablespoons olive oil in a large, heavy-based saucepan. Add 1 chopped onion and 1 chopped leek and cook for 5 minutes until softened. Pour in 1.2 litres (2 pints) hot vegetable stock and simmer for 5 minutes. Add 150 g (5 oz) asparagus tips and cook for 2 minutes, then add 75 g (3 oz) fozen peas and 100 g (3½ oz) ready-cooked rice. Season to taste. Heat through, ladle into bowls and serve sprinkled with chopped parsley and grated Parmesan cheese.

Fried Haloumi and Courgettes with Red Pepper Salsa

Serves 4

2 tablespoons olive oil

250 g (8 oz) baby courgettes, halved lengthways

200 g (7 oz) haloumi cheese, thickly sliced

salt and pepper

For the salsa

2 ready-roasted red peppers, finely chopped

1 garlic clove, crushed

1 red chilli, deseeded and finely chopped

finely grated rind and juice of ½ lemon

2 tablespoons extra virgin olive oil

handful of chopped mint

- Heat half the olive oil in a large frying pan. Add the courgettes and cook for 2 minutes, then turn over and cook for a further 1 minute until golden. Season to taste, remove from the pan and keep warm.

- Add the remaining olive oil to the pan, followed by the haloumi. Cook for 1–2 minutes on each side until golden.

- Meanwhile, mix together all the ingredients for the salsa. Divide the courgettes and haloumi between serving plates and spoon over the salsa to serve.

 Haloumi, Courgette and Red Pepper Kebabs Cut 200 g (7 oz) haloumi cheese, 2 large courgettes and 2 red peppers into large chunks. Toss with 2 tablespoons olive oil, season to taste and thread on to metal skewers. Heat a griddle pan until smoking hot. Split 4 pitta breads in half horizontally, then cut into 'chips'. Drizzle 2 tablespoons olive oil over the pitta chips and cook in the griddle pan for 1 minute until charred and lightly crisp. Remove from the pan and keep warm, then cook the kebabs in the pan for 3–5 minutes, turning occasionally, until golden. Meanwhile, toss a 400 g (13 oz) can chickpeas, rinsed and drained, with 1 small sliced red onion and a large handful of chopped basil and parsley. Drizzle with oil, season to taste and serve with the kebabs and pitta chips.

Roasted Haloumi and Courgette-Stuffed Peppers Cut 4 red or yellow peppers in half lengthways, remove the seeds and place on a baking sheet, cut sides up. Drizzle over 1 tablespoon olive oil and season well. Place in a preheated oven, 200°C (400°F), Gas Mark 6, for 10 minutes. Coarsely grate 2 small courgettes and mix with 1 beaten egg and 250 g (8 oz) ricotta cheese. Season and spoon into the peppers. Top the filling with a slice of haloumi and return to the oven for a further 10–15 minutes until golden and just set.

Beetroot Risotto with Goats' Cheese

Serves 4

1 tablespoon vegetable oil
1 onion, finely chopped
1 garlic clove, finely chopped
250 g (8 oz) risotto rice
100 ml (3½ fl oz) dry white wine
900 ml (1½ pints) hot vegetable
  stock
500 g (1 lb) cooked beetroot (not
  in vinegar), diced
25 g (1 oz) butter
100 g (3½ oz) goats' cheese
salt and pepper
handful of chopped dill, to garnish

- Heat the oil in a large, heavy-based saucepan. Add the onion and cook for 5 minutes until softened. Add the garlic and rice and cook for 30 seconds until coated in the oil. Pour in the wine and bubble until boiled away.

- Gradually add the stock, a ladleful at a time, stirring continuously and allowing each ladleful to be absorbed before adding the next. This should take about 15 minutes.

- Meanwhile, place half the beetroot in a food processor with a little of the stock and blend to a smooth purée.

- When the rice is nearly ready, add the diced and puréed beetroot. Cook for 2–3 minutes until the rice is tender, then stir in the butter, cover and leave to stand for 1 minute. Season to taste, then spoon into warmed bowls and serve scattered with the goats' cheese and dill.

 Beetroot and Grilled Goats' Cheese Salad Cut 75 g (3 oz) goats' cheese log into thick slices. Place on a greased baking sheet and cook under a preheated hot grill for 3 minutes until just golden and melted. Whisk 1 tablespoon sherry vinegar with 1 tablespoon finely chopped shallot and 3 tablespoons extra virgin olive oil. Season, then toss with 250 g (8 oz) diced cooked beetroot and 150 g (5 oz) mixed salad leaves. Divide between serving plates, then place the goats' cheese on top and sprinkle with 25 g (1 oz) roughly chopped walnuts.

Beetroot and Goats' Cheese Stacks Cut 250 g (8 oz) cooked beetroot into thin slices. Mix 75 g (3 oz) crème fraîche with 200 g (7 oz) soft goats' cheese until smooth. Lightly grease 4 x 7 cm (3 inch) ring moulds or large individual ramekins and place a slice of beetroot in the bottom of each. Spread a layer of the goats' cheese mixture on top, then add another slice of beetroot. Repeat the layers to use up the remaining ingredients. Place in a preheated oven, 180°C (350°F), Gas Mark 4, for 15–20 minutes until heated through. Turn out on to plates and serve with a green salad.

2 ⏱ Feta-Stuffed Peppers

Serves 4

1 tablespoon olive oil

4 long peppers

2 egg yolks

200 g (8 oz) feta cheese, crumbled

3 tablespoons natural yogurt

finely grated rind of ½ lemon

1 teaspoon chopped oregano

- Rub the oil over the peppers, arrange them in a grill pan and cook under a preheated hot grill for 5 minutes, turning once, until just soft. Leave to cool for a couple of minutes, then cut in half lengthways and remove the seeds.

- Place the egg yolks, three-quarters of the feta, the yogurt and lemon rind in a food processor and blend until smooth. Spoon the mixture into the peppers, then crumble the remaining feta on top and sprinkle with the oregano.

- Return to the grill and cook for 5–7 minutes until golden and cooked through. Leave to set for a couple of minutes before serving.

 Feta and Pepper Salad

Mash 100 g (3½ oz) feta cheese with 2 tablespoons double cream until well combined and smooth. Spoon the mixture over 4 ready-roasted pepper halves and roll up. Whisk 1 tablespoon lemon juice with 3 tablespoons olive oil and ½ teaspoon dried oregano, then season to taste. Toss together with 100 g (3½ oz) lambs' lettuce, ½ sliced cucumber and 50 g (2 oz) pitted black olives. Arrange the salad on a serving platter, cut the peppers into thick slices and arrange on top. Serve with crusty bread.

 Spicy Baked Feta with Peppers

Lightly grease 4 large sheets of foil. Divide 1 thinly sliced red onion between the sheets and top with 2 chopped ready-roasted peppers and a handful of halved cherry tomatoes. Place a 100 g (3½ oz) chunk of feta cheese on top of each portion and divide a handful of chopped oregano and 1 sliced red chilli between them. Drizzle over a little olive oil, then fold up the foil to make airtight parcels. Place on a baking sheet and cook in a preheated oven, 200°C (400°F), Gas Mark 6, for 20 minutes. Serve with plenty of crusty bread.

1 Thai Mixed Vegetable Soup

Serves 4

1 tablespoon vegetable oil
1 tablespoon Thai red curry paste
pinch of ground turmeric
150 ml (¼ pint) coconut milk
1 litre (1¾ pints) hot vegetable
  stock
1 lemon grass stalk
125 g (4 oz) baby sweetcorn
125 g (4 oz) shiitake mushrooms,
  halved
250 g (8 oz) ready-cooked rice
  noodles
125 g (4 oz) sugar snap peas
50 g (2 oz) bean sprouts
handful of chopped fresh coriander
lime wedges, to serve

· Heat the oil in a large, heavy-based saucepan. Add the curry paste and turmeric and cook for 1 minute, then stir in the coconut milk, stock and lemon grass and simmer for 2 minutes.

· Add the baby sweetcorn and mushrooms and cook for 2 minutes, then add the noodles and sugar snap peas and cook for a further 3 minutes. Ladle into warmed serving bowls and top with the bean sprouts. Sprinkle with the coriander leaves and serve with lime wedges.

2 Thai Mixed Vegetable Stir-Fry

Slice 125 g (4 oz) tofu and pat dry with kitchen paper. Heat 2 tablespoons oil in a wok. Add the tofu and stir-fry for 3 minutes until golden all over, then remove from the pan and set aside. Add more oil if necessary, then stir-fry 1 sliced onion for 2–3 minutes until softened. Stir in 1 teaspoon Thai red curry paste, 2 crushed garlic cloves and 2 teaspoons finely grated fresh root ginger. Stir for 1 minute, then add 1 cored, deseeded and sliced red pepper and 125 g (4 oz) each of mangetout and baby sweetcorn. Stir-fry for 3–4 minutes until tender, then return the tofu to the pan with 300 g (10 oz) ready-cooked rice noodles and 50 g (2 oz) bean sprouts. Pour in 2 tablespoons soy sauce and 1 tablespoon sweet chilli sauce and cook until the noodles have heated through, adding a little water if necessary. Serve with lime wedges.

3 Thai Mixed Vegetable Rice

Cook 1 finely chopped onion in 1 tablespoon oil for 5 minutes, then stir in 2 chopped garlic cloves and 1 tablespoon grated root ginger. Cook for 30 seconds, then stir in 1 tablespoon Thai red curry paste. Add 300 g (10 oz) basmati rice, 1 sliced red pepper and ½ diced Little Gem squash. Cook for 1 minute, then pour in 750 ml (1¼ pints) hot vegetable stock and 200 ml (7 fl oz) coconut milk. Cook for 10–12 minutes until most of the liquid is gone, then cover and cook over a low heat for 5 minutes until the rice is cooked through. Scatter with coriander.

ONE-VEGE-LOB

30 Red Pepper and Goats' Cheese Lasagne

Serves 4

butter, for greasing
2 ready-roasted red peppers, chopped
handful of chopped basil
500 ml (17 fl oz) ready-made tomato pasta sauce
125 g (4 oz) soft, rindless goats' cheese
150 g (5 oz) mascarpone cheese
5 tablespoons milk
8 fresh lasagne sheets
75 g (3 oz) ricotta cheese
25 g (1 oz) Parmesan cheese, grated
salt and pepper

- Lightly grease an ovenproof dish. Stir the red peppers and basil into the tomato sauce. Mix together the goats' cheese, mascarpone and milk and season to taste.

- Pour one-quarter of the tomato sauce in the ovenproof dish, then top with one-third of the goats' cheese mixture. Arrange a layer of pasta sheets on top. Repeat the layers until you have 3 layers of pasta, then spread the remaining tomato sauce on top.

- Spoon the ricotta over the sauce and scatter over the Parmesan. Place in a preheated oven, 200°C (400°F), Gas Mark 6, for 20–25 minutes until the pasta is tender.

 Spaghetti with Red Peppers and Goats' Cheese Cook 500 g (1 lb) quick-cook spaghetti in a large saucepan of lightly salted boiling water according to the pack instructions. Meanwhile, mix 2 chopped ready-roasted red peppers with 125 g (4 oz) soft goats' cheese, 50 g (2 oz) mascarpone cheese and a good handful of chopped parsley. Drain the pasta, return to the pan and stir in the sauce. Season to taste and serve sprinkled with toasted flaked almonds and chopped basil.

 Red Pepper Minestrone with Goats' Cheese Toasts Heat 2 tablespoons olive oil in a large, heavy-based saucepan. Add 1 finely chopped onion and cook for 5 minutes until softened, then stir in 2 cored, deseeded and chopped red peppers and 2 sliced garlic cloves. Cook for 1–2 minutes, then add 1.5 litres (2½ pints) hot vegetable stock and bring to the boil. Add 125 g (4 oz) soup pasta and cook for 5 minutes or according to the pack instructions. Slice a small baguette, toast the slices and spread with 75 g (3 oz) soft goats' cheese. Ladle the soup into warmed bowls, drizzle with 4 tablespoons fresh green pesto and serve with the toasts.

20 Spicy Paneer with Tomatoes, Peas and Beans

Serves 4

2 tablespoons vegetable oil
250 g (8 oz) paneer, diced
1 onion, finely chopped
2 garlic cloves, chopped
2 teaspoons finely grated fresh
  root ginger
1 teaspoon ground coriander
1 teaspoon paprika
1 teaspoon tomato purée
125 ml (4 fl oz) hot vegetable
  stock
150 g (5 oz) French beans
175 g (6 oz) frozen peas
150 g (5 oz) tomatoes, chopped
1 teaspoon garam masala
salt and pepper
chapattis, to serve

- Heat half the oil in a large frying pan. Add the paneer, season well and cook for 3–4 minutes until golden all over. Remove from the pan and set aside. Add the remaining oil to the pan with the onion. Cook for 5 minutes until softened, then add the garlic and ginger and cook for a further 1 minute. Add the spices and cook for 30 seconds.

- Stir in the tomato purée and stock and return the paneer to the pan with the beans. Season to taste, cover and simmer for 5 minutes. Add the peas and tomatoes and cook for a further 3 minutes, then stir in the garam masala. Divide between warmed bowls and serve with chapattis.

10 Spicy Paneer and Tomato Skewers Cut 250 g (8 oz) paneer into large cubes. Mix 1 teaspoon garam masala with ½ teaspoon cumin, a pinch of ground turmeric, a handful of chopped fresh coriander and 2 tablespoons vegetable oil. Toss with the paneer, then thread on to metal skewers with some whole cherry tomatoes. Season to taste. Heat a griddle pan until smoking hot, then cook the skewers for 3–5 minutes, turning once, until lightly charred. Serve with green salad and chapattis.

30 Spicy Paneer-Topped Peppers with Spinach and Peas Place 250 g (8 oz) chopped spinach in a sieve and pour over boiling water from the kettle until wilted, then squeeze thoroughly to remove excess water. Mix with 75 g (3 oz) frozen peas, 1 teaspoon each of ground cumin and ground coriander and 50 ml (2 fl oz) double cream and season to taste. Cut 2 red peppers in half lengthways and remove the seeds. Arrange on a lightly greased baking sheet and spoon the spinach mixture into the cavities. Slice 200 g (7 oz) paneer and arrange on top. Season well and drizzle with a little oil. Place in a preheated oven, 200°C (400°F), Gas Mark 6, for 20 minutes until bubbling. Finish off under the grill if the paneer is not browned.

Veggie Bean Chilli

Serves 4

2 tablespoons vegetable oil
1 onion, finely chopped
1 red pepper, cored, deseeded
and sliced
1 garlic clove, crushed
1 teaspoon ground cumin
1 teaspoon chipotle paste or
a pinch of chilli powder
1 teaspoon dried oregano
½ teaspoon ground coriander
400 g (13 oz) can chopped
tomatoes
400 g (13 oz) can black beans,
rinsed and drained
150 g (5 oz) canned sweetcorn,
drained
soured cream
handful of chopped fresh
coriander
grated Cheddar cheese
salt and pepper
tortilla chips, to serve

- Heat the oil in a large flameproof casserole dish. Add the onion and cook for 5 minutes until softened, then add the red pepper, garlic, spices and herbs and cook for 30 seconds. Pour in the tomatoes and season to taste. Bring to the boil, then reduce the heat and simmer for 10 minutes.

- Add the beans, sweetcorn and chocolate to the pan and cook for a further 3–4 minutes until heated through. Divide between warmed bowls and top each portion with a spoonful of soured cream. Sprinkle with the chopped coriander and grated cheese, then serve with tortilla chips.

 Chilli Bean Tostadas Cook 4 corn tortillas under a preheated hot grill for 2 minutes until crisp. Mix a 400 g (13 oz) can refried beans with 2 chopped tomatoes and a pinch of dried chilli flakes and spread over the tortillas. Scatter 75 g (3 oz) grated Cheddar cheese over the top and return to the grill for 3 minutes until the cheese melts. Serve topped with 1 sliced avocado and chopped coriander.

 Chilli Bean Empanadas Mix 200 g (7 oz) canned black beans, rinsed and drained, with 75 g (3 oz) canned sweetcorn, 2 finely chopped spring onions, 1 chopped tomato, ½ teaspoon ground cumin, a pinch of dried chilli flakes and 75 g (3 oz) grated Cheddar cheese. Roll out 300 g (10 oz) ready-made puff pastry on a lightly floured surface and cut out 4 rounds, 15 cm (6 inches) across. Arrange on a lightly greased baking sheet and divide the bean mixture between them, then brush around the edges with beaten egg. Fold the rounds in half to enclose the filling and use your fingers to crimp together the pastry to seal. Brush more egg over the parcels and cook in a preheated oven at 200°C (400°F), Gas Mark 6, for 20 minutes until puffed and golden.

 # Pizza Fiorentina

Serves 4

125 g (4 oz) baby spinach leaves
4 large wheat tortillas or flatbreads
150 ml (¼ pint) ready-made tomato sauce
125 g (4 oz) mozzarella cheese, sliced
4 eggs
25 g (1 oz) Parmesan cheese, grated

- Place the spinach in a sieve and pour over boiling water from the kettle until wilted, then squeeze thoroughly to remove excess water.

- Arrange the tortillas on 4 pizza trays. Spoon over the tomato sauce, then scatter over the spinach. Arrange the mozzarella on top, then crack an egg in the centre of each tortilla.

- Sprinkle the Parmesan over the pizzas, then place in a preheated oven, 220°C (425°F), Gas Mark 7, for 5–7 minutes until the egg whites are just set.

 Charred Tomato, Spinach and Tortilla Salad Cut 2 large tortillas or flatbreads into wedges. Brush with 1 tablespoon olive oil and place on a lightly greased baking sheet. Cook in a preheated oven, 200°C (400°F), Gas Mark 6, for 5 minutes until golden and crisp. Set aside and add 200 g (7 oz) cherry tomatoes to the baking sheet. Drizzle over a little more oil, season to taste and cook in the oven for 10 minutes until tender and lightly charred. Whisk 1 tablespoon balsamic vinegar with 3 tablespoons extra virgin olive oil and season to taste. Toss with 150 g (5 oz) baby spinach leaves and divide between serving plates.

Top with the tomatoes and tortilla wedges, then crumble over 75 g (3 oz) soft goats' cheese to serve.

 Tomato, Spinach and Tortilla Bake Place 400 g (13 oz) baby spinach leaves in a sieve and pour over boiling water from the kettle until wilted, then squeeze thoroughly to remove excess water. Mix with 250 g (8 oz) ricotta cheese and 75 g (3 oz) crumbled feta cheese. Divide between 8 small tortillas or flatbreads, roll up to enclose the filling and place in a lightly greased ovenproof dish, seam-side down. Pour over 500 ml (17 fl oz) ready-made tomato sauce and sprinkle with 125 g (4 oz) sliced mozzarella cheese and 50 g (2 oz) grated Cheddar cheese. Cook in a preheated oven, 190°C (375°F), Gas Mark 5, for 20 minutes until bubbling and golden.

3 Cauliflower Cheese with Leeks

Serves 4

1 cauliflower, cut into florets
1 large leek, sliced
500 ml (17 fl oz) hot vegetable
  stock
2 tablespoons cornflour
150 ml (¼ pint) crème fraîche
100 g (3½ oz) Cheddar cheese,
  grated
salt and pepper
crusty bread, to serve

- Place the cauliflower and leek in a shallow, flameproof casserole dish and pour in the stock. Cover and simmer for 5 minutes, then pour away half the stock.

- Transfer 3 tablespoons of the remaining stock to a cup and mix in the cornflour until smooth. Stir in the crème fraîche, then stir the mixture into the pan along with half the cheese. Cook for 1 minute, then season to taste.

- Sprinkle the remaining cheese over the vegetables and place in a preheated oven, 200°C (400°F), Gas Mark 6, for 15–20 minutes until golden and bubbling. Serve with crusty bread.

 Cauliflower and Blue Cheese Pasta

Cook 1 cauliflower, cut into florets, in a large saucepan of lightly salted boiling water for 8 minutes, then add 500 g (1 lb) fresh penne pasta and cook according to the pack instructions. Drain and return the cauliflower and pasta to the pan. Add 100 ml (3½ fl oz) crème fraîche and 75 g (3 oz) crumbled blue cheese. Stir until the cheese has melted, then serve immediately.

 Cauliflower Cheese Soup

Heat 2 tablespoons butter in a large, heavy-based saucepan. Add 1 chopped onion and cook for 5 minutes until softened. Add 1 cauliflower, broken into florets, 1 litre (1¾ pints) hot vegetable stock and 1 finely chopped sage leaf. Bring to the boil, reduce the heat and simmer for 10 minutes until the cauliflower is tender. Stir in 75 ml (3 fl oz) crème fraîche then use a hand-held electric blender to purée the soup until smooth. Stir in 50 g (2 oz) grated Cheddar cheese and serve with crusty bread.

ONE-VEGE-VUF

30 Pastry-Topped Summer Vegetables

Serves 4

5 tablespoons olive oil
2 courgettes, finely chopped
1 aubergine, finely chopped
1 red pepper, cored, deseeded
and thinly sliced
150 g (5 oz) ready-rolled puff
pastry
1 egg yolk
300 ml (½ pint) ready-made
tomato sauce
handful of basil leaves
25 g (1 oz) pitted black olives
salt and pepper

- Place the oil in a shallow ovenproof dish. Add the vegetables, toss to coat and season well. Place in a preheated oven, 220°C (425°F), Gas Mark 7, for 10 minutes, turning once, until golden.

- Meanwhile, cut the pastry into 4 rectangles and brush with the egg yolk. Stir the tomato sauce, basil and olives into the vegetables, then place a double layer of greaseproof paper on top.

- Place the pastry on top of the greaseproof paper and return the dish to the oven for 15 minutes until the pastry is golden and crisp. Slide the pastry off the paper to top the vegetables and serve immediately.

---

1 **Griddled Summer Vegetable Bruschetta** Toss 1 thinly sliced courgette and 2 cored, deseeded and sliced red peppers with 3 tablespoons olive oil. Cook in a smoking hot griddle pan for 3–5 minutes, turning once, until lightly charred. Season to taste and set aside to cool a little. Slice 1 baguette, toast the slices and rub with 1 peeled garlic clove. Mix 125 g (4 oz) ricotta cheese with a large handful of chopped basil and spoon over the toast. Arrange the vegetables on top, sprinkle with Parmesan shavings and serve immediately.

 Summer Vegetable Tart Place a sheet of ready-rolled puff pastry on a lightly greased baking sheet. Score around the edges with a knife to make a 1 cm (½ inch) border, then prick all over the centre with a fork. Arrange 3 chopped ready-roasted peppers, 125 g (4 oz) chopped ready-roasted aubergine and 1 thinly sliced courgette on top. Scatter over 150 g (5 oz) sliced mozzarella cheese and 25 g (1 oz) grated Parmesan cheese. Place in a preheated oven, 220°C (425°F), Gas Mark 7, for 15–17 minutes until golden and puffed. Drizzle with green pesto and serve with a rocket salad.

Tomato and Aubergine Pilaf

Serves 4

4 tablespoons olive oil

1 aubergine, diced

1 onion, finely chopped

1 tablespoon tomato purée

300 g (10 oz) coarse bulgar
  wheat, rinsed and drained

400 ml (14 fl oz) hot vegetable
  stock

400 g (13 oz) can chopped
  tomatoes

pinch of brown sugar

salt and pepper

natural yogurt, to serve

For the pesto

50 g (2 oz) toasted walnut pieces

1 garlic clove, crushed

bunch of parsley, chopped

4 tablespoons extra virgin olive oil

1 tablespoon capers, rinsed and
  drained

- Heat 3 tablespoons of the olive oil in a large, flameproof casserole dish. Add the aubergine and fry for 2–3 minutes until golden, then season to taste. Add the remaining oil to the pan along with the onion. Cook for 5 minutes until softened, then stir in the tomato purée.

- Add the bulgar wheat, stock, tomatoes and sugar. Bring to the boil, then cover the pan, reduce the heat and simmer gently for 15 minutes until the bulgar has absorbed all the liquid. Season to taste.

- Meanwhile, make the pesto. Place the walnuts in a food processor with the garlic, parsley and extra virgin olive oil. Blend to a smooth purée, then stir in the capers and season to taste. Divide the pilaf between serving plates and drizzle over the yogurt and pesto.

 **Tomato and Aubergine Bruschetta** Place 2 ready-roasted aubergines in a food processor with 75 ml (3 fl oz) natural yogurt, 1 crushed garlic clove and a handful of basil. Blend to form a smooth purée and season to taste. Thickly slice 1 baguette, lightly toast the slices and spoon the aubergine mixture on top. Scatter 2 chopped tomatoes and a few leaves of rocket over the bruschetta and serve immediately.

Tomato, Aubergine and Mozzarella Bake Slice 4 aubergines lengthways into long, thick slices, arrange in a lightly greased roasting tin and season well. Drizzle over 3 tablespoons olive oil, then place in a preheated oven, 220°C (425°F), Gas Mark 7, for 10 minutes. Turn the slices over and return to the oven for a further 5 minutes until golden. Pour over 250 ml (8 fl oz) passata or sieved tomatoes and scatter over 125 g (4 oz) chopped mozzarella cheese. Season to taste and cook for a further 10 minutes until bubbling and heated through. Scatter with basil leaves and serve with crusty bread and a green salad.

3 Baked Mushrooms with Goats' Cheese and Rocket

Serves 4

500 g (1 lb) new potatoes, halved
3 tablespoons olive oil
200 g (7 oz) portobello
  mushrooms
2 tablespoons chopped thyme
6 garlic cloves, unpeeled
50 g (2 oz) soft goats' cheese
125 g (4 oz) cherry tomatoes
25 g (1 oz) toasted pine nuts
75 g (3 oz) rocket
salt and pepper

· Toss the potatoes with 2 tablespoons olive oil and place in a large, shallow roasting tin. Place in a preheated oven, 220°C (425°F), Gas Mark 7 for 15 minutes, turning once.

· Add the mushrooms, stem side up, thyme and garlic to the tin, drizzle over the remaining oil and season well. Place a little goats' cheese on each mushroom and return to the oven for a further 5 minutes.

· Add the cherry tomatoes and return to the oven for a further 5 minutes more until the potatoes and mushrooms are cooked through. Scatter over the pine nuts and serve with the rocket.

 Mushroom, Goats' Cheese and Rocket Omelettes Heat a little butter in a frying pan. Add 150 g (5 oz) sliced mushrooms and cook for 2 minutes, then add 1 crushed garlic clove and cook for a further 1 minute until tender. Remove from the pan and set aside. Beat 5 eggs with 25 g (1 oz) finely chopped rocket and season to taste. Melt a little more butter in the pan, add one-quarter of the egg mixture, swirl around and cook for 1 minute until just set. Scatter over one-quarter of the mushrooms and a little goats' cheese, then roll up and keep warm. Repeat with the remaining ingredients to make 4 omelettes in all, then serve with crusty bread.

 Mushroom Burgers with Goats' Cheese and Rocket Place 4 large portobello mushrooms on a lightly greased baking sheet. Season well, then place in a preheated oven, 220°C (425°F), Gas Mark 7, for 15 minutes or until tender. Split and lightly toast 4 ciabatta rolls. Place a mushroom on the bottom half of each roll, then divide 50 g (2 oz) soft goats' cheese, 4 tablespoons fresh green pesto and 1 thinly sliced tomato between them. Replace the tops and serve with a rocket salad.

Wintery Minestrone with Pasta and Beans

Serves 4

2 tablespoons olive oil
1 onion, chopped
1 celery stick, chopped
1 carrot, chopped
1 garlic clove, crushed
400 g (13 oz) can chopped
  tomatoes
1.5 litres (2½ pints) vegetable
  stock
1 rosemary sprig
150 g (5 oz) small soup pasta
75 g (3 oz) cavolo nero or other
  cabbage
200 g (7 oz) canned cannellini
  beans, rinsed and drained
4 tablespoons fresh green pesto
25 g (1 oz) Parmesan cheese,
  grated
salt and pepper
crusty bread, to serve

- Heat the oil in a large, heavy-based saucepan. Add the onion, celery and carrot and cook for 5 minutes until softened, then add the garlic and cook for a further 1 minute. Pour in the tomatoes and stock, add the rosemary and bring to the boil. Reduce the heat and simmer for 15 minutes.

- Add the pasta and cabbage and cook for 5–7 minutes, or according to the pack instructions. Stir in the beans and heat through, then season to taste. Ladle the soup into warmed bowls, drizzle with the pesto, sprinkle with the Parmesan and serve with crusty bread.

 Pasta and Bean Salad
Cook 300 g (10 oz) orzo pasta in a large saucepan of lightly salted boiling water for 5 minutes. Drain, cool under cold running water and drain again. Toss with 200 g (7 oz) canned cannellini beans, rinsed and drained, 150 g (5 oz) halved cherry tomatoes and 125 g (4 oz) rocket. Stir in 4 tablespoons extra virgin olive oil and 1 tablespoon white wine vinegar, season to taste and serve sprinkled with grated Parmesan.

 Spring Vegetable Minestrone with Beans Heat 1 tablespoon olive oil in a large, heavy-based saucepan. Add 1 chopped onion and cook for 5 minutes until softened. Stir in 1 crushed garlic clove and cook for 30 seconds. Pour in 1.5 litres (2½ pints) hot vegetable stock and the rind of ½ lemon, pared in wide strips, and simmer for 5 minutes. Remove the strips of lemon rind and add 200 g (7 oz) canned cannellini beans, rinsed and drained, 1 finely chopped courgette and 150 g (5 oz) peas or French beans. Simmer for 3–5 minutes until the vegetables are just tender, then stir in a handful of chopped basil and serve with crusty bread.

3⬤ Courgette and Ricotta Bakes

Serves 4

butter, for greasing
2 courgettes
100 g (3½ oz) fresh white
   breadcrumbs
250 g (8 oz) ricotta cheese
75 g (3 oz) Parmesan cheese,
   grated
2 eggs, beaten
1 garlic clove, crushed
handful of chopped basil
salt and pepper

- Lightly grease 8 holes in a large muffin tin. Use a vegetable peeler to make 16 long ribbons of courgette and set aside. Coarsely grate the remainder of the courgettes and squeeze to remove any excess moisture.

- Mix the grated courgette with the remaining ingredients and season well. Arrange 2 courgette ribbons in a cross shape in each hole of the muffin tin. Spoon in the filling and fold over the overhanging courgette ends.

- Place in a preheated oven, 190°C (375°F), Gas Mark 5, for 15–20 minutes, or until golden and cooked through. Turn out on to serving plates.

 1 Penne with Courgettes and Ricotta Cook 500 g (1 lb) fresh penne pasta in a large saucepan of lightly salted boiling water according to the pack instructions, adding 75 g (3 oz) frozen peas for the last 2 minutes of cooking. Drain and return the pasta and peas to the pan. Add the finely grated rind of 1 lemon and 2 tablespoons lemon juice. Use a vegetable peeler to slice 2 courgettes into long ribbons. Add to the pan with 50 g (2 oz) rocket, 2 tablespoons olive oil and 25 g (1 oz) grated Parmesan cheese. Season to taste, divide between bowls and top with a spoonful of ricotta cheese.

 2 Mushrooms Stuffed with Courgettes and Ricotta Brush a little olive oil over 4 large field mushrooms and place on a baking sheet, stem side up. Grate 1 courgette and squeeze to remove any excess moisture, then mix with 200 g (7 oz) ricotta cheese, 4 chopped sun-dried tomatoes and 25 g (1 oz) chopped pitted black olives. Season and spoon on to the mushrooms, then sprinkle with 25 g (1 oz) grated Parmesan cheese. Place in a preheated oven, 200°C (400°F), Gas Mark 6, for 15 minutes until golden and cooked through. Serve with ciabatta rolls.

ONE-VEGE-TIQ

3⬤ Tortilla with Sun-Blush Tomato and Rocket Salad

Serves 4

4 tablespoons olive oil
1 onion, finely chopped
3 potatoes, thickly sliced
200 ml (7 fl oz) water
5 eggs, beaten
75 g (3 oz) rocket
2 tablespoons extra virgin olive oil
2 tablespoons lemon juice
50 g (2 oz) sun-blush tomatoes
handful of Parmesan cheese
  shavings
salt and pepper

- Heat the olive oil in a large, nonstick frying pan. Add the onion and potato and cook for 5–10 minutes until golden, then pour in the measurement water. Simmer gently until the potatoes are very tender, then pour away any excess liquid.

- Season the eggs well, then pour into the pan and stir gently. Cook over a gentle heat for 10–15 minutes until set all the way through, finishing off under a preheated grill to set the top if necessary.

- Toss the rocket with the extra virgin olive oil, lemon juice and tomatoes. Season well and add the Parmesan shavings. Cut the tortilla into wedges and serve topped with the salad.

 Egg, Tomato and Rocket Wraps
Crack 4 eggs into a lightly greased, nonstick frying pan. Dot with 50 g (2 oz) mascarpone cheese and season well. Cook over a gentle heat for 2–3 minutes until starting to set. Stir in 1 chopped tomato and cook for a further 1 minute until just set. Spoon over 4 wheat tortilla wraps, then scatter with 50 g (2 oz) rocket and a little crumbled goats' cheese. Wrap up the tortillas and serve.

 Baked Eggs with Spicy Tomato and Rocket Sauce Mix 300 ml (½ pint) ready-made tomato sauce with 75 g (3 oz) roughly chopped rocket and a pinch of dried chilli flakes. Spoon into 4 greased ramekins. Crack an egg into each ramekin, drizzle over a little olive oil and scatter with some grated Parmesan cheese. Place in a preheated oven, 200°C (400°F), Gas Mark 6, for 15 minutes or until the eggs are just set.

ONE-VEGE-CEF

Spicy Sweet Potato and Feta Salad

Serves 4

5 tablespoons olive oil

2 sweet potatoes, thinly sliced

1 tablespoon white wine vinegar

150 g (5 oz) baby spinach leaves

1 tablespoon finely chopped
   red onion

125 g (4 oz) feta cheese, crumbled

1 red chilli, sliced

50 g (2 oz) pitted black olives

salt and pepper

- Toss 2 tablespoons of the oil with the sweet potatoes. Season well and cook in a preheated hot griddle pan for 3 minutes on each side until tender and lightly charred.

- Meanwhile, mix together the remaining oil with the white wine vinegar and season to taste. Toss with the spinach and red onion and arrange on serving plates. Arrange with the sweet potatoes, feta, chilli and olives and serve immediately.

 Baked Sweet Potatoes with Spicy Feta Filling Pierce 4 large sweet potatoes 2 or 3 times with a fork. Microwave on medium power for 5 minutes until starting to soften. Rub all over with 2 teaspoons olive. Place in a preheated oven, 220°C (425°F), Gas Mark 7, for 10–15 minutes until the skin is crisp and the potatoes cooked through. Cut a cross in each potato, open out and divide 50 g (2 oz) feta cheese, 50 g (2 oz) rocket, 1 finely chopped red chilli and 25 g (1 oz) sliced black olives between them. Drizzle with olive oil and serve immediately.

 Spicy Sweet Potato and Feta Bake Place 875 g (1¾ lb) peeled and sliced sweet potatoes in a shallow, flameproof casserole dish with 300 ml (½ pint) double cream and 1 deseeded and finely chopped red chilli. Season to taste and simmer for 15 minutes until tender. Meanwhile, place 200 g (7 oz) spinach in a sieve and pour over boiling water from the kettle until wilted, then squeeze thoroughly to remove excess water. Stir into the dish. Scatter over 50 g (2 oz) dried white breadcrumbs and 75 g (3 oz) crumbled feta cheese. Drizzle with 2 tablespoons olive oil, then cook under a preheated hot grill for 3 minutes until golden.

QuickCook
Puddings

Recipes listed by cooking time

30

20

10

 # Crunchy Berry Brûlée

Serves 4

250 g (8 oz) mascarpone cheese
300 ml (½ pint) ready-made
  fresh custard
150 g (5 oz) mixed berries
100 g (3½ oz) caster sugar
1½ tablespoons water

- Beat the mascarpone until smooth, then gently stir in the custard and transfer the mixture to a serving dish. Scatter the berries on top.

- Place the sugar and measurement water in a small, heavy-based saucepan and slowly bring to the boil, carefully swirling the pan from time to time. Keep cooking until the sugar dissolves, then turns a deep caramel colour. Pour over the berries and leave for a few minutes to harden.

 ### Peach and Berry Cream Crunch

Peel, stone and chop 2 peaches and arrange in a shallow, flameproof dish, then scatter over 125 g (4 oz) mixed berries. Spoon over 300 g (10 oz) crème fraîche, then top with 100 g (3½ oz) demerara sugar to completely cover the crème fraîche. Place as close as you can to a preheated very hot grill and cook for 2–3 minutes until the sugar has caramelized.

 ### Melting Berry Yogurt

Place 200 g (7 oz) mixed berries in a serving dish. Spoon over 300 ml (½ pint) natural yogurt, then sprinkle with 75 g (3 oz) soft dark brown sugar. Chill in the refrigerator for 20–25 minutes until the sugar has melted.

ONE-PUDD-DUG

30 Apple and Orange Tart

Serves 4

300 g (10 oz) ready-rolled puff pastry

5 apples, such as Coxes, cored and thinly sliced

6 tablespoons caster sugar

finely grated rind of 1 orange

- Place the pastry on a baking sheet and use a sharp knife to lightly score a 1 cm (½ inch) border round the edges, taking care not to cut right through the pastry. Prick all over the centre of the pastry with a fork.

- Toss the apples with 5 tablespoons of the sugar and the orange rind, then arrange on top of the pastry. Sprinkle over the remaining sugar. Place in a preheated oven, 220°C (425°F), Gas Mark 7, for 20 minutes until the apples are tender and the pastry is crisp.

 Apple and Orange Compote

Heat 25 g (1 oz) butter in a frying pan. Add 2 peeled, cored and sliced apples and cook for 3 minutes, stirring frequently. Stir in 2 tablespoons caster sugar and the finely grated rind and juice of 1 orange. Continue to cook for about 5 minutes until the apples are tender and the sauce is syrupy. Mix ½ teaspoon ground cinnamon with 150 ml (¼ pint) natural yogurt and serve with the compote.

 Apple and Orange Brioche Tarts

Cut out a round from each of 4 slices of brioche, using a cup as a guide. Butter both sides and arrange on a baking sheet. Mix 25 g (1 oz) ground almonds and 4 tablespoons caster sugar with 3 tablespoons mascarpone cheese and the finely grated rind of ½ orange, then spoon on to the brioche. Arrange 2 cored and thinly sliced apples on top, then sprinkle over 2 tablespoons caster sugar. Place in a preheated oven,

200°C (400°F), Gas Mark 6, for 15–20 minutes until golden.

 # Strawberry Cream Puffs

Serves 4

300 g (10 oz) ready-rolled
  puff pastry
4 tablespoons icing sugar
300 ml (½ pint) double cream
300 g (10 oz) strawberries, hulled
  and halved

- Cut the pastry into 12 equal rectangles and arrange on a baking sheet, then place another baking sheet on top. Place in a preheated oven, 200°C (400°F), Gas Mark 6, for 10 minutes until golden and crisp.

- Sift half the icing sugar over the pastry puffs and cook under a preheated hot grill for 30 seconds until the sugar melts. Leave to cool.

- Whisk the cream with the remaining icing sugar until soft peaks form. Arrange the pastry strips, whipped cream and strawberries on plates and serve immediately.

 ### Strawberry Cream Pots

Whisk 300 ml (½ pint) double cream with ½ teaspoon vanilla extract and 2 tablespoons icing sugar until soft peaks form. Stir in 200 g (7 oz) hulled and chopped strawberries and divide between small glass bowls. Serve with shortbread biscuits.

 ### Strawberry Cream Tart

Spread 4 tablespoons strawberry jam over the base of a shop-bought, ready-made sweet tart case. Whisk 300 ml (½ pint) double cream with 3 tablespoons icing sugar, 4 eggs and 1 teaspoon vanilla extract and pour into the tart case. Place in a preheated oven, 180°C (350°F), Gas Mark 4, for 25 minutes, until golden and just set. Scatter with hulled and chopped strawberries to serve.

Syrup Sponge Pudding

Serves 6

175 g (6 oz) butter, softened, plus extra for greasing

175 g (6 oz) caster sugar

175 g (6 oz) self-raising flour

1 teaspoon baking powder

3 eggs

1 teaspoon vanilla extract

3 tablespoons milk

finely grated rind of ½ lemon

6 tablespoons golden syrup

cream or custard, to serve

- Grease a 1.2 litre (2 pint) pudding basin. Place all the ingredients, except the golden syrup, in a food processor and blend until smooth. Spoon 4 tablespoons of the golden syrup into the bottom of the basin, then add the pudding mixture and smooth the surface with a knife.

- Cover with microwave-proof clingfilm and pierce the film a couple of times with a sharp knife. Cook in a microwave oven on medium heat for about 12 minutes. Test to see if it is cooked by inserting a skewer into the pudding; it should come out clean.

- Leave to rest for 3 minutes, then turn out on to a deep plate and spoon over the remaining golden syrup. Serve with cream or custard.

 Syrup-Topped Hotcakes

Place 200 g (7 oz) self-raising flour in a food processor with 1 teaspoon baking powder, 2 eggs, 250 ml (8 fl oz) milk and a pinch of salt and blend until smooth. Heat a large, nonstick frying pan. Add a little butter and swirl around the pan, then add generous tablespoonfuls of the batter. Cook for 2 minutes until starting to set, then turn over and cook for a further 1 minute. Remove from the pan, keep warm and repeat with the remaining batter. Serve the cakes scattered with blueberries and drizzled generously with golden syrup.

 Syrup Sponge Puddings with Ginger Make the sponge pudding mixture following the main recipe, adding 1 teaspoon ground ginger. Generously grease 6 dariole moulds, individual pudding basins or ramekins with butter and place a small circle of greaseproof paper in the bottom of each. Mix 4 tablespoons golden syrup with 2 teaspoons chopped stem ginger and a little of the syrup from the jar. Spoon into the moulds and top with the pudding mixture. Place in a preheated oven, 180°C (350°F), Gas Mark 4, for 15–20 minutes until cooked through and springy to

the touch. Leave in the moulds for 3 minutes, then turn out on to serving plates and serve drizzled with more golden syrup.

 # Cinnamon-Spiced Cherries

Serves 4

25 g (1 oz) caster sugar
350 ml (12 fl oz) rosé wine
strip of pared lemon rind
1 cinnamon stick
500 g (1 lb) cherries, pitted
  if liked

- Combine all the ingredients in a saucepan. Bring to the boil, then reduce the heat and simmer for 5 minutes until the sugar has dissolved and the cherries are tender.

- Use a slotted spoon to transfer the cherries to a serving dish, then cook the liquid over a high heat for 3–4 minutes until syrupy. Remove the cinnamon and lemon rind, then pour over the cherries and serve warm or cold.

 ## Cherry and Cinnamon Soup

Heat 450 ml (¾ pint) fruity white wine in a saucepan with 75 g (3 oz) caster sugar, 1 cinnamon stick, 1 strip of pared orange rind and a good squeeze of juice. Simmer for 10 minutes, then add 500 g (1 lb) pitted cherries and cook for 5 minutes until tender. Remove the orange rind and cinnamon, add 150 ml (¼ pint) mascarpone cheese and purée with a hand-held electric blender until smooth. Add a few ice cubes to cool the soup, then spoon into serving bowls and scatter with chocolate shavings and a few more pitted cherries.

 ## Cherry and Cinnamon Biscuits

Beat 250 g (8 oz) softened butter with 150 g (5 oz) caster sugar. Stir in 1 egg yolk, then fold in 300 g (10 oz) plain flour and 1 teaspoon ground cinnamon. Finally add 50 g (2 oz) dried cherries. Divide into 12 large balls and place on a baking sheet lined with greaseproof paper, well spaced apart. Bake in a preheated oven, 180°C (350°F), Gas Mark 4, for 12–15 minutes until just cooked. Leave to cool on a wire rack, then serve sandwiched together with scoops of vanilla ice cream.

30 Chocolate Fudge Brownie

Serves 8

200 g (7 oz) butter
200 g (7 oz) dark chocolate, chopped
175 g (6 oz) soft dark brown sugar
150 g (5 oz) caster sugar
4 eggs, beaten
50 g (2 oz) ground almonds
75 g (3 oz) plain flour
vanilla ice cream, to serve

- Gently melt the butter and chocolate in an ovenproof frying pan, about 23 cm (9 inches) across. Remove from the heat and cool for a couple of minutes.

- Beat together the sugars and eggs, then stir in the chocolate mixture followed by the almonds and flour.

- Wipe the rim of the frying pan with a damp piece of kitchen paper to neaten, then pour the mixture into the pan. Place in a preheated oven, 180°C (350°F), Gas Mark 4, for 25 minutes until just set. Serve warm with vanilla ice cream.

 Malted Brownie Sundaes

Bring 150 ml (¼ pint) double cream to the boil in a small, heavy-based saucepan. Remove from the heat and stir in 100 g (3½ oz) chopped dark chocolate until smooth. Cut 200 g (7 oz) shop-bought brownie into small squares and place in the bottom of sundae glasses. Add 2 scoops of vanilla ice cream to each glass, then drizzle over the chocolate sauce. Roughly crush 50 g (2 oz) Maltesers and scatter over the top to serve.

 Brownie Lollipop Bites

Press 250 g (8 oz) shop-bought brownie into 20 small balls. Spear each one on a thin lollipop stick and place in the freezer for 10 minutes to firm up. Bring 100 ml (3½ fl oz) double cream to the boil in a small, heavy-based saucepan. Remove from the heat and stir in 50 g (2 oz) chopped chocolate until smooth. Dip the lollipops in the melted chocolate, transfer to a baking sheet lined with greaseproof paper and let cool and harden.

Tropical Fruit Salad

Serves 4

2 lemon grass stalks, roughly chopped
150 ml (¼ pint) water
150 g (5 oz) caster sugar
125 g (4 oz) pineapple, peeled and sliced
1 mango, peeled and sliced
½ papaya, peeled and chopped
coconut macaroons, to serve

- Place the lemon grass, measurement water and sugar in a small, heavy-based saucepan, bring to the boil and cook for 1 minute. Transfer to the freezer until cool, about 10 minutes.

- Arrange the fruit in a serving bowl. Strain the syrup over the fruit and serve with macaroons or coconut ice cream.

Tropical Fruit with Lemon Sugar

Mix 25 g (1 oz) demerara sugar with the finely grated rind of 1 lemon and a handful of chopped mint. Arrange a mixture of peeled and sliced tropical fruits on serving plates, then scatter over the sugar to serve.

Sticky Coconut Rice with Tropical Fruit Cook 200 g (7 oz) pudding rice in a large saucepan of boiling water according to the pack instructions. Transfer to a colander to drain. Add 100 g (3½ oz) coconut cream, 3 tablespoons caster sugar and 1 lemon grass stalk to the pan and heat through. Return the rice to the pan, stir well and set aside for 10 minutes to cool. Peel and cut 1 mango and ½ pineapple into thin slices and serve with the coconut rice, topped with a sprinkling of desiccated coconut.

ONE-PUDD-BIX

Rum and Raisin French Toast

Serves 4

4 eggs, beaten
1 teaspoon vanilla extract
75 ml (3 fl oz) single cream
4 tablespoons rum
½ teaspoon ground cinnamon
4 thick slices of raisin bread,
  halved
25 g (1 oz) butter

- Mix together the eggs, vanilla extract, cream, rum and cinnamon. Dip the raisin bread slices in the mixture and leave to soak for 2 minutes.

- Heat a large, nonstick frying pan. Add a little butter and swirl around the pan. Cook the bread for 2–3 minutes on each side until golden.

 Rum and Raisin Banana Sundaes

Soak 25 g (1 oz) raisins in 4 tablespoons rum. Place 100 g (3½ oz) caster sugar in a small, heavy-based saucepan. Bring to the boil over a low heat, then simmer until it starts to turn a dark caramel colour. Remove from the heat. Carefully add 50 ml (2 fl oz) double cream (it will spit), followed by the rum and raisin mixture. Return to the heat and stir until smooth. Halve 4 bananas lengthways and arrange in serving bowls. Scoop some vanilla ice cream on top, then pour over the rum and raisin sauce.

 Rum and Raisin Apple Charlotte

Peel, core and chop 4 small apples and mix with 5 tablespoons ready-made apple sauce, 2 tablespoons rum and 25 g (1 oz) raisins. Place in a shallow ovenproof dish, cover with foil and cook in a preheated oven, 200°C (400°F), Gas Mark 6, for 15 minutes until the apples are tender. Butter 6 slices of brioche and cut in half, then remove the foil and arrange over the apples. Sprinkle over 50 g (2 oz) demerara sugar, then return to the oven for 10 minutes until crisp.

30 Rhubarb and Ginger Slump

Serves 4–6

750 g (1½ lb) rhubarb, trimmed
and cut into chunks
1 tablespoon self-raising flour
50 g (2 oz) granulated sugar
2 pieces of stem ginger in syrup,
drained and chopped, plus
2 tablespoons syrup from the jar

Topping

100 g (3½ oz) self-raising flour
75 g (3 oz) butter, softened
75 g (3 oz) granulated sugar
4 tablespoons milk
1 egg, beaten

- Place the rhubarb, flour, sugar and ginger in a shallow ovenproof dish and toss together. Cover with foil and place in a preheated oven, 190°C (375°F), Gas Mark 5, for 3 minutes.

- Meanwhile, place the ingredients for the topping in a food processor and blend until smooth. Uncover the rhubarb and spoon over the topping.

- Return to the oven for a further 25 minutes or until the topping is golden and cooked through.

 Rhubarb and Ginger Fools

Whisk 200 ml (7 fl oz) double cream until soft peaks form, then stir in 1 tablespoon icing sugar. Gently stir in 125 g (4 oz) canned rhubarb, drained and chopped, and divide between serving bowls. Crumble 1 ginger biscuit over each portion and serve immediately.

 Rhubarb and Ginger Cream Baskets Stir 40 g (1½ oz) melted butter with 50 g (2 oz) caster sugar, 1½ tablespoons golden syrup, ½ tablespoon double cream and 40 g (1½ oz) plain flour until smooth. Drop tablespoonfuls of the mixture, well spaced apart, on a baking sheet lined with greaseproof paper. Place in a preheated oven, 180°C (350°F), Gas Mark 4, for 5–10 minutes until golden. Remove from the oven and drape the biscuits over lightly oiled teacups while they are still hot. Leave until crisp and set. Whisk 150 ml (¼ pint) double cream until soft peaks form, then stir in 1 chopped piece of stem ginger and 1 tablespoon syrup from the jar. Spoon into the baskets, top each with a spoonful of canned rhubarb and serve immediately.

Choc-Chip Ice Cream Sandwiches

Serves 4 (with leftover cookies)

150 g (5 oz) butter, softened

100 g (3½ oz) granulated sugar

100 g (3½ oz) soft light brown sugar

1 egg, beaten

175 g (6 oz) plain flour

1 teaspoon baking powder

1 teaspoon vanilla extract

100 g (3½ oz) mixed dark, milk and white chocolate chips

4 scoops of vanilla ice cream

- Line a baking sheet with greaseproof paper. Beat the butter and sugars until light and fluffy, then stir in the egg. Beat in the flour, baking powder and vanilla extract, then stir in three-quarters of the chocolate chips.

- Use a teaspoon to dollop 24 walnut-sized balls of dough, well spaced apart, on to the baking sheet and flatten gently. Scatter with the remaining chocolate chips and cook in the preheated oven, 190°C (375°F), Gas Mark 5, for 8–10 minutes until golden and just cooked through.

- Leave the cookies to cool on a wire rack, then serve 2 to each person, sandwiched together with a scoop of vanilla ice cream.

Quick Choc-Chip Ice Cream Sandwiches with Chocolate Sauce Sandwich together 8 ready-made choc-chip cookies in pairs with 4 scoops of vanilla ice cream. Bring 150 ml (¼ pint) double cream to the boil in a small, heavy-based saucepan, then pour over 2 tablespoons caster sugar and 100 g (3½ oz) chopped dark chocolate in a heatproof bowl. Stir until smooth, then drizzle over the sandwiches to serve.

 Choc-Chip Scone Sandwiches Mix 450 g (14½ oz) self-raising flour in a mixing bowl with 1 tablespoon caster sugar, 1 teaspoon bicarbonate of soda and a pinch of salt. Rub in 100 g (3½ oz) diced cold butter with fingertips until the mixture resembles fine breadcrumbs. Stir in 300 ml (½ pint) buttermilk and 75 g (3 oz) chocolate chips. Bring the dough together, then turn out on to a lightly floured surface and press down until uniformly about 3 cm (1¼ inches) thick. Cut out scones with a 5 cm (2 inch) round cutter, piling up and pressing down the trimmings to cut out more scones. Place on a lightly floured baking sheet, brush with beaten egg yolk and cook in a preheated oven, 220°C (425°F), Gas Mark 7, for 12–15 minutes until cooked through. Leave to cool. Whisk 300 ml (½ pint) double cream until soft peaks form, then stir in 1 teaspoon vanilla extract and icing sugar to taste. Split the scones and fill with the cream to serve.

ONE-PUDD-RUX

Baked Figs with Honey and Pistachios

Serves 4

12 figs

25 g (1 oz) butter, plus extra for greasing

2 tablespoons soft light brown sugar

2 tablespoons runny honey

3 tablespoons orange juice

½ teaspoon ground cinnamon

25 g (1 oz) shelled unsalted pistachio nuts

natural yogurt, to serve

- Lightly grease a small, shallow roasting tin. Cut a cross down into the top of each fig, then arrange them in the tin. Place a little butter on each, then pour over the sugar, honey, orange juice and cinnamon.

- Place in a preheated oven, 200°C (400°F), Gas Mark 6, for 12 minutes, then scatter over the pistachios and return to the oven for a further 3 minutes until the figs are tender. Serve with natural yogurt.

Grilled Figs with Honey Mascarpone and Pistachio Biscotti Cut 12 figs in half and arrange, cut sides up, on a grill pan. Place a little piece of butter on top of each and sprinkle over ½ teaspoon ground cinnamon. Cook under a preheated hot grill for 5 minutes until tender. Mix 150 g (5 oz) mascarpone cheese with 1 tablespoon runny honey and ½ teaspoon vanilla extract. Serve the hot figs with the mascarpone and some pistachio biscotti.

Fig, Honey and Pistachio Tarts Cut out 4 rounds about 12 cm (5 inches) across from a 375 g (13 oz) pack ready-rolled puff pastry. Arrange on a lightly greased baking sheet and crimp the edges. Process 75 g (3 oz) shelled unsalted pistachio nuts in a blender until smooth, then mix with 1 egg yolk, 1 tablespoon soft light brown sugar and 1 tablespoon runny honey. Spread the mixture over the centres of the pastries, then arrange 2 sliced figs on top of each. Place in a preheated oven, 220°C (425°F), Gas Mark 7, for 20 minutes until golden and cooked through. Drizzle over a little more honey to serve.

ONE-PUDD-FYZ

1 Chocolate Fondue with Marshmallows

Serves 4

300 ml (½ pint) double cream
2 tablespoons orange liqueur
  (optional)
150 g (5 oz) dark chocolate,
  chopped
150 g (5 oz) milk chocolate,
  chopped
marshmallows, biscuits and mini
  doughnuts, to serve

- Bring the cream to the boil in a small, heavy-based saucepan. Remove from the heat and stir in the liqueur, if using, and the chocolate until melted. Transfer to a warmed serving bowl or fondue pot, if liked.

- Arrange the marshmallows, biscuits and mini doughnuts on a serving plate, spear them on long forks and dip them into the warm chocolate.

---

2 Chocolate and Marshmallow

Trifle Place 150 g (5 oz) mini marshmallows, 50 g (2 oz) butter and 250 g (8 oz) chopped chocolate in a heavy-based saucepan and melt over a low heat until smooth. Stand the pan in a bowl of cold water and leave to cool for 5–10 minutes. Whisk 250 ml (8 fl oz) double cream until it holds its shape, then stir in 1 teaspoon vanilla extract and the cooled chocolate mixture. Arrange bite-sized chunks of plain cake in the bottom of a serving dish and spoon the chocolate mixture on top. Scatter over a handful of raspberries and blueberries to serve.

3 Chocolate Cupcakes with

Melting Marshmallows Place 150 g (5 oz) light brown muscovado sugar, 100 g (3½ oz) self-raising flour, 50 g (2 oz) cocoa powder and 1 teaspoon baking powder in a large bowl. Stir in 3 eggs, 125 ml (4 fl oz) vegetable oil, 2 tablespoons milk and 50 g (2 oz) chocolate chips. Spoon the mixture into a 12 hole bun tray lined with cupcake cases. Place in a preheated oven, 180°C (350°F), Gas Mark 4, for 20 minutes. Top the cupcakes with 25 g (1 oz) mini marshmallows and place under a preheated hot grill for 1 minute until lightly charred.

 **Boozy Caramelized Oranges**

Serves 4

4 oranges
200 g (7 oz) caster sugar
4 tablespoons water
3 tablespoons orange liqueur

- Peel the oranges and cut into thick slices, reserving any juice. Place the sugar in a heavy-based saucepan with the measurement water. Cook over a medium heat until it starts to turn a dark brown colour.

- Remove from the heat and carefully pour in the liqueur (it will spit). The caramel will harden, so return to a low heat and cook until melted again. Stir in the oranges and any juice, then spoon into glass bowls and serve.

 Boozy Caramel and Orange Trifle

Cook 200 g (7 oz) sugar and 5 tablespoons water in a heavy-based saucepan until golden brown. Remove from the heat, add 25 g (1 oz) butter and 200 ml (7 fl oz) double cream and set aside to cool. Whisk 250 ml (8 fl oz) double cream with 3 tablespoons icing sugar until soft peaks form. Cut 150 g (5 oz) trifle sponges into pieces and arrange in the bottom of a serving bowl. Pour over 50 ml (2 fl oz) orange juice and 1 tablespoon orange liqueur. Spoon the cream on top. Arrange 2 oranges, peeled and cut into segments, over the cream, then drizzle over the caramel sauce. Serve sprinkled with toasted almonds.

Crêpes Suzette

Place 150 g (5 oz) plain flour, 200 ml (7 fl oz) milk, 1 egg and a pinch of sugar in a food processor and blend until smooth. Heat a nonstick frying pan and add a little butter. Swirl around the pan, then add a ladleful of batter. Cook for 1 minute until set, then turn over and cook for 30 seconds more. Fold into quarters, set aside and repeat with the remaining batter. Add 50 g (2 oz) caster sugar and 3 tablespoons water to the frying pan and cook until the sugar turns golden. Remove from the heat, add 150 ml (¼ pint) fresh orange juice and 2 tablespoons orange liqueur. Return to a low heat and cook until smooth, then add the folded crêpes and heat through, spooning over the sauce.

30 Tiramisu

Serves 4

200 ml (7 fl oz) double cream
50 ml (2 fl oz) marsala
250 g (8 oz) mascarpone cheese
4 tablespoons icing sugar
1 teaspoon vanilla extract
300 ml (½ pint) very strong
  coffee, cooled
20 sponge fingers
25 g (1 oz) dark chocolate, grated,
  to decorate

- Whisk the cream until stiff peaks form. Reserve 1 tablespoon of the marsala, then stir the remaining marsala into the cream with the mascarpone, 3 tablespoons of the icing sugar and the vanilla extract.

- Stir the remaining marsala and icing sugar into the coffee, then dip 4 of the sponge fingers into the mixture and place each in the bottom of a glass or small serving dish. They should be just soft, not soggy.

- Spoon some of the creamy mixture on top, then repeat the layers to use up the remaining ingredients. Chill in the refrigerator for 20 minutes, then serve sprinkled with grated chocolate.

 **Creamy Coffee Martinis**
Whisk 125 ml (4 fl oz) double cream with 2 tablespoons marsala until slightly thickened. Stir together 250 ml (8 fl oz) cooled coffee with 6 tablespoons coffee liqueur and 1 tablespoon icing sugar. Pour into 4 cocktail glasses, top with the thickened cream, then grate over a little chocolate and serve with sponge fingers.

2 Tiramisu Cupcakes
Place 100 g (3½ oz) each of butter, soft light brown sugar and self-raising flour in a food processor with 1 egg, 1 egg yolk and 75 ml (3 fl oz) cooled strong coffee and blend until smooth. Spoon the mixture into a 12-hole muffin tray lined with paper cupcake cases and place in a preheated oven, 180°C (350°F), Gas Mark 4, for 15–18 minutes until a skewer inserted into the cakes comes out clean.

ONE-PUDD-BYK

Prune Clafoutis

Serves 4

butter, for greasing
3 eggs
125 g (4 oz) caster sugar
50 g (2 oz) plain flour
150 ml (¼ pint) double cream
150 ml (¼ pint) milk
1 teaspoon vanilla extract
75 g (3 oz) pitted soft prunes

- Lightly grease a shallow ovenproof dish. Whisk together the eggs and sugar until pale, frothy and tripled in volume. Sift the flour into the bowl and lightly fold in. Add the cream, milk and vanilla extract and mix until just combined.

- Pour into the ovenproof dish and place in a preheated oven, 190°C (375°F), Gas Mark 5, for 5 minutes until the surface is just starting to set. Scatter over the prunes, then return to the oven for a further 15–20 minutes until the clafoutis is risen and golden.

---

1 **Creamy Plum and Port Fools**

Whisk 300 ml (½ pint) double cream until soft peaks form, then stir in 50 ml (2 fl oz) port, 6 stoned and chopped plums and a little caster sugar, to taste. Divide the creamy mixture between serving glasses.

 Plum Crisp

Halve and stone 200 g (7 oz) plums and place in a lightly greased ovenproof dish. Cut 25 g (1 oz) butter into small pieces and scatter over the plums with 2 tablespoons caster sugar. Cover with foil and place in a preheated oven, 200°C

(400°F), Gas Mark 6, for 10 minutes. Meanwhile, crush 125 g (4 oz) ginger biscuits and mix with 25 g (1 oz) softened butter. Remove the foil and scatter the biscuit mixture over the plums. Return to the oven for a further 5 minutes until lightly crisp.

Passionfruit and Mango Mess

Serves 4

300 ml (½ pint) double cream
2–3 tablespoons icing sugar
4 meringue nests, crushed
1 mango, peeled and sliced
1 passionfruit, halved

- Whisk the cream with the icing sugar until it just holds its shape. Gently stir in the meringue, most of the mango and a little of the passionfruit pulp. Spoon into glasses and top with the remaining fruit.

 ### Passionfruit and Mango Cream

Peel and chop 1 mango and divide between 4 glasses. Whisk 1 egg yolk with 2 tablespoons caster sugar until very frothy and pale, then stir in the pulp of 2 passionfruit. Whisk 200 ml (7 fl oz) double cream until soft peaks form, then stir into the egg mixture and whisk until thickened. Add 1 tablespoon orange liqueur and 75 g (3 oz) crushed meringues. Spoon over the mango and top with a little more chopped fruit, if liked.

Passionfruit Meringue Puddings

Bring 150 ml (¼ pint) single cream and 250 ml (8 fl oz) milk to the boil in a heavy-based saucepan. Meanwhile, whisk 4 egg yolks with 75 g (3 oz) caster sugar. Carefully stir in the hot milk, then add 125 g (4 oz) fresh white breadcrumbs and the pulp of 4 passionfruit. Divide between 4 x 200 ml (7 fl oz) ramekins and place in a preheated oven, 160°C (325°F), Gas Mark 3, for 20 minutes until just set. Meanwhile, whisk the

4 egg whites until stiff, then slowly whisk in 50 g (2 oz) caster sugar until glossy and smooth. Spoon over the puddings and return to the oven for 3–5 minutes until lightly golden.

ONE-PUDD-KOR

30 Peach and Raspberry Melba

Serves 4

250 ml (8 fl oz) water
125 g (4 oz) caster sugar
1 vanilla pod
4 peaches, halved and stoned
8 scoops of vanilla ice cream
125 g (4 oz) raspberries
biscuit curls, to serve

- Place the measurement water, sugar and vanilla extract in a saucepan, cook over a low heat until the sugar dissolves, then cook over a high heat for 5–10 minutes until syrupy.

- Add the peach halves and cook for a further 5 minutes until tender, then leave to cool. Remove the skins and thinly slice the peaches.

- Arrange the peach slices, ice cream and half the raspberries in sundae glasses. Press the remaining raspberries through a sieve to make a coulis, drizzle over the top of the sundaes and serve with biscuit curls.

 Caramelized Peaches with Mascarpone and Raspberries

Tightly fit 4 halved and stoned peaches into an ovenproof dish, cut sides up. Sprinkle with 2 tablespoons caster sugar, then place 1 tablespoon mascarpone cheese into the hollow of each peach half. Scatter over 75 g (3 oz) raspberries, followed by another 2 tablespoons sugar. Cook under a preheated hot grill for 3–5 minutes until golden and bubbling.

 Baked Peaches and Raspberries

Place 4 halved and stoned peaches in an ovenproof dish. Pour over 6 tablespoons orange juice and add 2 tablespoons orange liqueur, if liked. Dot a little butter on each peach, then sprinkle with 2 tablespoons caster sugar. Place in a preheated oven, 200°C (400°F), Gas Mark 6, for 15 minutes, then scatter over 100 g (3½ oz) raspberries and return to the oven for a further 3 minutes until tender and lightly caramelized. Serve with vanilla ice cream.

ONE-PUDD-NYK

3 Apricot and Almond Crostata

Serves 6–8

butter, for greasing
icing sugar, for dusting
250 g (8 oz) shortcrust pastry
150 g (5 oz) marzipan, sliced
8 apricots, halved and stoned
25 g (1 oz) flaked almonds
2 tablespoons milk
2 tablespoons caster sugar
cream or custard, to serve

- Lightly grease a baking sheet. Dust a work surface with icing sugar, then roll out the pastry into a 35 cm (14 inch) round. Place on the baking sheet, arrange the marzipan slices in the middle and top with the halved apricots.

- Scatter the almonds over the top, then fold the edges of the pastry up and over to form a rough border. Brush the pastry border with the milk and sprinkle with the caster sugar. Place in a preheated oven, 200°C (400°F), Gas Mark 6, for 25 minutes until the pastry is just cooked through. Serve with cream or custard.

 Apricot and Almond Pots

Place 200 g (7 oz) apricots in a small saucepan with 125 ml (4 fl oz) apple juice and heat until softened. Break 100 g (3½ oz) almond biscotti into small pieces and place in serving glasses. Spoon over the warmed apricots along with a little almond liqueur, if liked. Top with 150 g (5 oz) thick natural yogurt and a handful of toasted almond flakes.

 Baked Apricots Stuffed with Almonds Place 125 g (4 oz) amaretti biscuits in a food processor with 25 g (1 oz) blanched almonds, 1 egg white and 2 tablespoons sugar and pulse to form a rough paste. Halve 9 apricots, and arrange cut sides up in a shallow ovenproof dish, then place a little of the almond mixture on top of each apricot. Place in a preheated oven, 200°C (400°F), Gas Mark 6, for 10–15 minutes until the fruit is tender and the topping is crisp.

3⦿ Creamy Chocolate Puddings

Serves 4

75 g (3 oz) granulated sugar
3 tablespoons cornflour
25 g (1 oz) cocoa powder
3 eggs
500 ml (17 fl oz) milk
75 g (3 oz) milk chocolate,
  chopped

To serve

whipped cream
grated chocolate

- Place the sugar, cornflour and cocoa powder in a heatproof bowl and whisk in the eggs. Bring the milk to the boil in a saucepan, then whisk a little of it into the egg mixture. Transfer the chocolate mixture to the saucepan, stir well and cook for 3–5 minutes, stirring continuously, until thickened.

- Place the chopped chocolate in the bowl, sieve the chocolate custard on top and stir until smooth. Cover the surface with clingfilm to prevent a skin forming, then place in the freezer for 15 minutes, stirring occasionally, until cool.

- When the chocolate custard is cool, divide between glass bowls, top with whipped cream and sprinkle with grated chocolate.

 1⦿ Creamy Chocolate Sauce with Brioche Dunkers Bring 150 ml (¼ pint) double cream to the boil in a small, heavy-based saucepan. Remove from the heat, add 100 g (3½ oz) chopped dark chocolate and stir until smooth. Halve 4 brioche rolls and lightly toast. Butter well and sprinkle with ½ teaspoon ground cinnamon. Dunk the brioche in the chocolate sauce to serve.

 2⦿ Creamy Chocolate Truffles Bring 75 ml (3 fl oz) double cream to the boil in a small, heavy-based saucepan. Place 150 g (5 oz) chopped dark chocolate in a heatproof bowl with 25 g (1 oz) butter. Pour over the cream and stir until smooth. Place in the freezer for 15 minutes, stirring occasionally, until the mixture has set. Use a teaspoon to scoop out pieces of the mixture, form into balls and roll in cocoa powder to serve.

Banana and Caramel Puffs

Serves 4

150 g (5 oz) soft light brown sugar

50 ml (2 fl oz) water

25 g (1 oz) butter

300 g (10 oz) ready-rolled puff pastry

2 bananas, sliced

- Heat the sugar and measurement water in a large ovenproof frying pan until golden and caramel coloured. Carefully add the butter and swirl around the pan until melted.

- Meanwhile, cut out 4 rounds from the pastry using a 7 cm (3 inch) cookie cutter.

- Carefully arrange the banana slices in 4 circles in the caramel, then place a pastry round on top of each. Place in a preheated oven, 220°C (425°F), Gas Mark 7, for 15 minutes until puffed and cooked through. Use a spatula to turn out of the pan and drizzle with the remaining sauce.

 Banana and Caramel Pots

Slice 2 bananas and divide between glass serving bowls. Whisk 150 ml (¼ pint) double cream until soft peaks form, then stir in 1 tablespoon dulce de leche or other caramel sauce. Spoon over the banana, then drizzle with more dulce de leche and top with chopped pecans.

 Banana and Caramel Tart

Lay 300 g (10 oz) ready-rolled puff pastry on a work surface, place an ovenproof frying pan on top and cut around it, leaving a 2 cm (¾ inch) border. Chill in the refrigerator until ready to use. Heat 150 g (5 oz) soft light brown sugar in the frying pan with 100 ml (3½ fl oz) water until the sugar melts and starts to turn golden. Remove from the heat. Halve 3 or 4 bananas lengthways and arrange in the pan until the bottom is almost covered. Lay the pastry on top and tuck in the edges. Place in a preheated oven, 220°C (425°F), Gas Mark 7, for 20 minutes or until golden and puffed.

30 Apple and Blackberry Strudels

Serves 4

75 g (3 oz) butter, melted
3 Granny Smith apples, peeled, cored and thinly sliced
125 g (4 oz) blackberries
100 g (3½ oz) caster sugar
pinch of ground cinnamon
4 large sheets of filo pastry
icing sugar, for dusting
clotted cream, to serve

- Mix together the apples, blackberries, sugar and cinnamon. Unwrap the filo pastry and cover with a piece of damp kitchen paper until ready to use it.

- Working quickly, brush 1 sheet of pastry with the butter and arrange one-quarter of the apple mixture in a sausage shape along one short side, leaving a 2.5 cm (1 inch) space at each end. Fold the 2 long sides in over the mixture, then roll up the pastry to enclose it completely. Repeat with the remaining ingredients to make 4 rolls in all.

- Place the strudels on the baking sheet and cook in a preheated oven, 200°C (400°F), Gas Mark 6, for 15–20 minutes until crisp. Serve with clotted cream.

---

1 Apple and Blackberry Fools

Whisk 300 ml (½ pint) double cream until soft peaks form. Stir in 100 ml (3½ fl oz) good-quality, ready-made apple sauce. Spoon into serving dishes, top with a few blackberries and dust with icing sugar.

2 Crunchy Apple and Blackberry Crumble

Peel, core and chop 4 apples. Place in an ovenproof dish and stir in the finely grated rind of 1 lemon, 50 g (2 oz) caster sugar, 1 teaspoon vanilla extract and 4 tablespoons water. Cover with foil and place in a preheated oven, 190°C (375°F), Gas Mark 5, for 15 minutes. Remove the foil, add 125 g (4 oz) blackberries and return to the oven for a further 1 minute. Meanwhile, lightly crush 100 g (3½ oz) crumbly butter biscuits, scatter over the fruit and return to the oven for 1–2 minutes until crisp.

1⃝ Lemon Syllabub

Serves 4

300 ml (½ pint) double cream
75 ml (3 fl oz) sweet white wine
50 g (2 oz) caster sugar
finely grated rind and juice of
  ½ lemon

- Whisk the cream until it just starts to hold its shape. Add the wine, one-third at a time, whisking well between each addition.

- Stir in the sugar and lemon juice and continue whisking until fluffy and thick. Spoon into glasses, scatter with lemon rind and serve.

---

 2 Lemon Cheesecake Pots with Blueberries Place 125 g (4 oz) blueberries in a small saucepan with 3 tablespoons caster sugar and 2 tablespoons water and cook until the berries start to burst. Leave to cool. Meanwhile, mix 250 g (8 oz) mascarpone cheese with 3 tablespoons icing sugar and 2 tablespoons lemon juice. Crush 4 digestive biscuits and divide between glasses, then spoon the lemon mixture on top. Pour over the cooled blueberries and their juice and serve.

 3 Little Lemon Puddings Beat 50 g (2 oz) butter and 75 g (3 oz) caster sugar with the finely grated rind of 1 lemon until light and fluffy. Add 2 egg yolks and 4 tablespoons lemon juice. Stir in 1 tablespoon flour, then 100 ml (3½ fl oz) double cream and 150 ml (¼ pint) milk until smooth. Pour into 4 lightly greased 200 ml (7 fl oz) ramekins. Place the ramekins in a shallow roasting tin and pour boiling water into the tin until it comes halfway up the ramekins. Place in a preheated oven, 180°C (350°F), Gas Mark 4, for 20–25 minutes until golden and slightly risen.

3⊙ Crunchy Pear Crumble

Serves 6

6 pears, peeled, cored and
chopped
2 tablespoons soft light brown
sugar
½ teaspoon ground cinnamon
4 tablespoons water
custard, to serve

Topping

75 g (3 oz) soft light brown sugar
½ teaspoon ground cinnamon
125 g (4 oz) rolled oats
75 g (3 oz) plain flour
75 g (3 oz) butter
1 tablespoon golden syrup

- Place the pears in a shallow ovenproof dish with the sugar, cinnamon and measurement water and stir together. Cover with foil and place in a preheated oven, 190°C (375°F), Gas Mark 5, for 5 minutes.

- Meanwhile, make the crumble topping. Place the sugar in a food processor with the cinnamon, oats, flour and butter and pulse until the mixture resembles fine breadcrumbs. Alternatively, rub the butter into the dry ingredients with your fingertips. Stir the golden syrup into the topping mixture.

- Remove the pears from the oven, uncover and scatter the topping over them. Return to the oven for a further 20–25 minutes or until bubbling and lightly browned. Serve warm with custard.

 Sautéed Pears with Crunchy Topping

Heat 25 g (1 oz) butter in a frying pan. Add 6 pears, peeled, quartered and cored, and cook for 5 minutes, turning often, until golden all over. Stir in ½ teaspoon ground cinnamon and 6 tablespoons orange juice and cook until the liquid bubbles away. Divide between serving dishes, then scatter with 6 crushed flapjack biscuits mixed with 25 g (1 oz) chopped pecan nuts. Spoon over natural yogurt or whipped cream to serve.

 Pear Crumble Tarts

Cut out 6 x 10 cm (4 inch) rounds from 2–3 sheets of ready-rolled puff pastry, arrange on a lightly greased baking sheet and place a thinly sliced pear on each one. Place 75 g (3 oz) plain flour in a mixing bowl with 75 g (3 oz) sugar, 25 g (1 oz) flaked almonds and ½ teaspoon ground cinnamon. Rub in 75 g (3 oz) diced butter with fingertips and scatter over the pears. Cook in a preheated oven, 220°C (425°F), Gas Mark 7, for 15 minutes until puffed and golden.

 # Vanilla Zabaglione

Serves 4

6 egg yolks
50 g (2 oz) caster sugar
1 vanilla pod
4 tablespoons marsala or
 dessert wine
biscotti, to serve

- Place the egg yolks and sugar in a heatproof bowl. Split the vanilla pod lengthways, scrape out the seeds, add to the bowl and whisk together. Place the bowl over a saucepan of gently simmering water, taking care that the bottom of the bowl does not touch the water.

- Add the marsala and whisk continuously with a hand-held electric whisk for 5–8 minutes until the mixture is frothy and thickened. It should leave a trail when you remove the beaters. Pour into glass serving bowls and serve with biscotti.

 Vanilla Egg Nog

Bring 500 ml (17 fl oz) milk and 200 ml (7 fl oz) single cream to the boil in a heavy-based saucepan with 1 split vanilla pod. Beat 4 egg yolks with 75 g (3 oz) caster sugar in a heatproof bowl to combine, then pour on the hot milk and stir well. Return to the pan and cook over a low heat for 5–10 minutes until thickened. Place 125 g (4 oz) chopped white chocolate in the mixing bowl with 2 tablespoons brandy, if liked. Pour over the thickened milk and stir until combined. Spoon into cups to serve.

 Vanilla Zabaglione Cream

Make the Vanilla Zabaglione, as above, then chill in the refrigerator for 15 minutes. Whisk 200 ml (7 fl oz) double cream until soft peaks form, then carefully stir in the cooled zabaglione. Transfer to a serving dish, scatter with fresh raspberries and serve with tuille biscuits.

Index

Page references in *italics* indicate photographs

Acknowledgements

Recipes by **Emma Lewis**
Executive Editor **Eleanor Maxfield**
Editor **Alex Stetter**
Copy Editor **Jo Smith**
Art Direction **Tracy Killick for Tracy Killick Art Direction and Design**
Original Design Concept www.gradedesign.com
Designers **Tracy Killick and Janis Utton for Tracy Killick Art Direction and Design**
Photographer **William Shaw**
Home Economists **Emma Jane Frost, Emma Lewis**
Stylist **Liz Hippisley**
Senior Production Controller **Caroline Alberti**